You are Enough

How to elevate your thoughts,
align your energy and get out
of the comparison trap

Cassie Mendoza-Jones

HAY
HOUSE

Copyright © 2016 Cassie Mendoza-Jones

Published and distributed in Australia by: Hay House Australia Pty. Ltd.: www.hayhouse.com.au
Published and distributed in the United States by: Hay House, Inc.: www.hayhouse.com
Published and distributed in the United Kingdom by: Hay House UK, Ltd.: www.hayhouse.co.uk
Published and distributed in South Africa by: Hay House SA (Pty), Ltd.: www.hayhouse.co.za
Distributed in Canada by: Raincoast Books: www.raincoast.com
Published in India by: Hay House Publishers India: www.hayhouse.co.in

Design by Rhett Nacson
Custom Cover Typography by Dani Hunt
Typeset by Bookhouse, Sydney
Edited by Margie Tubbs
Author photo by Bayleigh Vedelago

ISBN: 978-1-4019-5066-8

1ˢᵗ edition, April 2016

To my parents, Marylou and Robin, my sisters,
Steph and Sami, and my hubby, Nic.

One word: Love.

Praise for *You Are Enough*

'As a recovering perfectionist, this is the book I wish I'd read years ago when my inner saboteur was the boss of me. Cassie will teach you how to self soothe and stop pushing yourself to exhaustion. Pause, take a breath and read!'

—Amy Molloy, Journalist, Author & Contributing Editor at
The Collective magazine

'Cassie's beautiful book will help women end the tirade that we so often have with our inner critic, and get to a place of peace and self love. Sound grand? It is a grand journey, but through Cassie's beautiful words and wisdom, she makes it seem possible for women to find their confidence, get the most from their energy, and finally realise their self-worth. This book will help change many lives'.

—Megan Dalla-Camina, *Getting Real About Having It All*

'As a former perfectionist, Cassie's book spoke to me from the very first page. As I move forward in my personal development journey, I understand that our only job is to gently and lovingly release our inner self-critic and give ourselves permission to be ... enough. Cassie has curated some brilliant tools to help you release those blocks, to allow ourselves to be perfectly imperfect.'

—Denise Duffield-Thomas, Money Mindset Mentor,
www.LuckyBitch.com

'Cassie has created a wonderful guide with **You Are Enough**, full of practical life advice and soulful insights. It is sure to resonate strongly with many people, as it has done for me!'

–Kathleen Murphy, Naturopath, Medical Writer, Educator & Author

'**You Are Enough** is a true gem that helps you become "besties" with your inner-critic and adopt beautiful self-care practices to feed your soul. This is the book you'll refer to again and again – letting the edges curl from wear, highlighting your favorite passages, and feverishly scribbling notes in the margins. Cassie shares how to plug up your leaky energy from worrying, comparing and despairing and helps you unpack old attitudes and mindsets that no longer serve. This book will claim a proud spot in my library for life.'

–Melissa Cassera, Business Strategist & Screenwriter

'Cassie does a wonderful job in **You Are Enough** of connecting the physical, mental, emotional and spiritual components of self-worth, helping the reader to clear limiting beliefs and blocks, revealing the perfect, whole being you've always been in the process. Cassie's toolkit steps the reader through change from a place of loving acceptance, rather than a place of pushing to be something other than the perfection you already are. A great addition to any self-empowerment bookshelf.'

–Helen Jacobs, Founder and Channel at The Little Sage

'This book is the book every single woman on this planet needs to read. Cassie artfully articulates exactly what is going through our minds – the societal pressure to be something we're not – and skillfully provides the means to overcome this. Each word is laced with love, each sentence loaded with care. I can guarantee it will be filled with highlighted notes and little heart scribbles in no time.'

–Kate Toholka, *Healthy Habits*

'**You are Enough** is a deep dive into learning how to raise your own spirits, be your own cheerleader and grow your self-love and resilience. It's perfect for anyone who has ever experienced self-doubt or worried they're not good enough. Cassie is a truly wonderful guide, full of deep wisdom and loving suggestions to help you on your path. Rich with stories any young woman can relate to and practical exercises to help you action what you're learning, **You Are Enough** is a book you will love and return to again and again whenever you need a boost to your confidence.'

–Kerry Rowett, Kinesiologist, Awaken Kinesiology

'Abundance is deeply linked with healthy self-worth. Cassie's identification of several ways that low self-worth prevents abundance is refreshingly clear. She walks her readers through potential issues in the most compassionate way, and best of all, offers practical solutions borne from her personal experience. This is a simple and effective "how to" guide for cultivating self-esteem and enjoying life!'

–Ezzie Spencer PhD, creator of *Lunar Abundance*

'Cassie's beautiful creation **You Are Enough** will take you on a journey that traverses through the most common (but paralysing) blocks that keep us feeling flat, burnt out, unworthy and 'less than'. And while it lovingly sheds light on these facets, **You Are Enough** then paves a clear path out of the woods, towards a life that feels free, flowing, and luminously on your own terms. It is a journey rich in self-discovery, of multiplying self-love, and uncovering and nurturing your acceptance of you (just as you are!).'

–Claire Murray, Naturopath & Writer

'**You Are Enough** is a beautiful read for anyone who wants to boost their thoughts and energy to live a confident and happy life. Cassie is a champion for women's self-care and nourishment and her writing is so fresh and engaging that while reading, you feel like you're getting (great) advice from a knowledgeable girlfriend who wants the absolute best for you. If you're ready to step up in your life and your relationship with yourself, I'd highly recommend picking up a copy of Cassie's book, locking your door and reading from cover to cover!'

–Hayley Richardson, Writer at www.HayleyRichardson.co

Contents

Part Three
intuition, wisdom, guidance

Part Four
cleansing, balancing + aligning your energies

Part Five
your energetic toolkit

Concluding Pages

foreword

by Alice Nicholls

✺

irstly, I am honoured to be writing a foreword to a book which I know would have changed my life for the better, some years ago. There are feelings of both nostalgia, at remembering the young woman I was who desperately needed what's within these very pages and hope, because it's finally here for all of those women who desperately need it now. And it's oh so required.

In my early twenties, after I had dragged myself through too-many-to-count, sick-inducing hangovers trying to fit in; after my thousandth deprivation diet had resulted in a binge through another bag of sweets, sitting in my car in my pajamas, in a 7-Eleven car park at 10am; after I had almost resigned myself to not being good enough to keep the man or attract the man; and right on the cusp of my sinking into career despair, because I didn't know what I wanted to be when I 'grew up', I began living my life as this very book coaches you to consider living your life.

What I found amid my own chaos of confusion, self-doubt, comparison and struggle was that I was truly a woman to be reckoned with.

I found both my peace and personal success through that journey to find myself—as clichéd as that may sound; it's a cliché because it's true. However I was so very close to missing the chance to meet the woman I am proud to be now, just as I know many of you who open this book are also close to believing that the empowered and at peace woman doesn't exist within you.

Now as a successful businesswoman, writer, nutritionist, coach and mentor, who has been able to meet with and speak to hundreds of women who were walking in shoes that closely resembled mine back then, I know how painfully uncomfortable many of our current generation are.

There has never been a generation as empowered as ours. We are emerging from repression around our careers, our sexuality, our choices and gaining a voice.

And here is the biggest paradox of our generation in the 21st century: we have never been so empowered, have never had such a loud voice and a dizzying number of opportunities, yet at the same time we are crushed by our own fear, anxiety, stress and belief that we are less than, not enough or simply not worthy of greatness ... even when it is all laid out on a platter waiting for us to come and claim it.

The beauty, fashion and fitness industries, with the clever marketing that comes along for the ride, have brought us to our knees. We are a generation who are not repressed by society but by ourselves, as a result of trying to live up to a perceived expectation of what society wants us to be. It's a perpetual and damaging cycle ... and we keep buying into it.

Both men and women today are growing up and entering adulthood with a scarcity mindset, thinking we are never smart enough, powerful enough, rich enough or skinny enough.

We want the perfect careers, the perfect hair, the perfectly-styled apartments, and the most expensive car. We always want to eat the healthiest food, have the most disciplined exercise regimes and, of course, the fittest, most perfect body.

We also want the world to find us attractive enough, and we'll go to many damaging lengths to feel like we are.

We (just) want to be an A+ juggler of it all. This shouldn't be too hard, right?

We are also stunted in our personal growth because we place such high pressure on how we're perceived in the world. We ask, 'Are my contributions meaningful enough?' We live in a culture which says that if we're not doing extraordinary things—if we're just living an 'ordinary' life —this is synonymous with living a meaningless life.

Many of us are no longer measuring ourselves against our own experiences, but measuring ourselves against our sisters, mothers, fathers, friends, colleagues and of course, the millions of strangers we will never know, but whose curated lives we can access at the touch of a button.

As much as we believe we're aware of what everyone else thinks of us, we're also becoming more and more disconnected ... with work, family and ourselves.

We need guidance to find our way out of this. Now.

Before we met in 'real life', I met Cassie online, as many people do today. Believe me when I say, Cassie sparkles! You'll find in the coming pages that she lights a spark in you too.

We formed a friendship through a shared message in support of all of us reaching our full potential. The potential that has nothing to do with the results of a cleanse or a diet or an exercise regime fit for the army, but the potential which can only be unlocked when we connect to ourselves on a much deeper level.

While Cassie didn't know me as that lost young women I spoke of, she knew me in the way someone can know somebody else because they've had hundreds of variations of that person sit across from them in their practice, sharing their struggles with food, body image, nourishment, comparison, anxiety, dis-ease with life, health concerns and feelings of not belonging.

It's not very often that you're able to tap into the knowledge of a highly-respected and regarded nutritionist, naturopath, kinesiologist, coach and speaker all within a single book. To know that this book is finally going to be available to all women who need it most is incredibly soothing to me, as a fellow practitioner in this industry who knows how desperately needed this is.

You Are Enough is significant in that Cassie writes from personal experience and also as a qualified professional in her numerous fields. She has lived and implemented her own strategies and expertise, before bringing them to the table for you to benefit from. She has encountered the problem and also brings the solution.

In a world where we sometimes simply want to be able to hear someone say 'me too', this is extremely comforting.

Cassie has easily tapped into what our own inner negative voice sounds like, in a conversational, easily understood style, so much so that at times I truly felt like I had my own sassy coach sitting over my shoulder, reading along with me and nodding, 'Yes, me too'.

Unlike many books in the self-help space, Cassie has been able to weave questions, projects and tasks for us to undertake throughout her debut book. So instead of coming away with just a 'thought', we come away having been asked to play a role in our own positive change.

In *You Are Enough*, Cassie gently requests that we activate ourselves to our truest potential. It takes more than a yoga class, a green smoothie or a single session of meditation to undo what has potentially been years of stress, anxiety, fear, 'busyness' and self-loathing and reach that potential. *You Are Enough* is a 'doing' book, and one thing I know for sure is that you can't elevate yourself without doing.

An individual resolution to drop the constant strive to be seen as worthy or perfect or enough by others is a grand place to start. And so, with this book you're in the right place.

And hey, if you ever needed proof that the message in this book works, look to the author herself, who has personally worked though anxiety, comparison, stress and busy-ness and come out the other side a better woman. However she doesn't stop there, as we now know. She writes the freakin' book about it and changes the world!

There is a peaceful leader within you that you may not have found yet. So know that your energy is about to be raised. You're not perfect, struggle is going to come up in your life, but it's going to be beautiful and you're in the right place.

Alice Nicholls
Founder of *The Whole Daily*
Writer, Nutritionist, Coach and Mentor

introduction

✖

I've written and rewritten this first line a dozen times. That's because you only get one chance to craft the opening lines in your first book, and there are just so many ways to begin. From the tender age of about twelve, I knew I'd be an author one day (hello, inner guide!), hence for years I've imagined writing this introduction to you. Today I finally get to begin.

Only a couple of years ago, my inner perfectionist and personal critic would have ranted and raged at me to create the most perfect opening line in the history of opening lines of first books. And while I used to listen to her and bend to her unkind ways, we now have a strange and wonderful sort of relationship; I can acknowledge her need for perfection and balance it with my need for momentum, ease and grace.

I realised the best way to start this book was to simply start this book, knowing that what I ended up writing would be the right thing to write. Before we dive into it, I want you to know that making friends with your inner critic (who tells you that you'll never be enough) is possible for you too. Helping you see that is one of the reasons I wrote this book.

If you're a perfectionist too, if you always listen to your inner critic who tells you you're not good enough and that you never will be, if you constantly worry about everything and wonder what people are thinking of you, and if you never trust yourself or know how to listen to and follow your own guidance, you're in the right place. I've been there, and now I want to help you find your own deep sense of acceptance and confidence, because I know that you're worthy of it.

As I write this, I'm sitting by the fireplace in a quaint lounge room in a hotel in Carmel, California. I am make-up free, which feels a little remarkable. It's not the fact that I'm on holiday in Carmel that's remarkable (although the view is!), rather it's the fact that I feel completely safe, comfortable and confident, sitting here with freshly-washed hair and a make-up free face.

A few years ago, I would never have left the house with wet hair, or hair that wasn't straightened, without some bronzer, mascara and eyeliner. (What would people think of me?)

Am I able to do this now because I care less about my appearance? Oh, no. I'm able to do this because I care **more** for my sense of self-worth and I know that, make-up or no make-up, I'm still worthy. I know that my worth isn't tied up in the things I do, the way I look, or what I eat for breakfast.

I know that the way I accept myself is up to one person, and that person is me. I know that I don't need to prove myself with silky, straight hair (although that's lovely), or glossy, dewy skin (another great thing) or with the yoga pants that I also wore yesterday (oops, they're comfy, what can I say?).

I know that my worth is innate, I know that your worth is innate. And I know that when you can start to accept yourself more deeply, more fully, more unconditionally, you'll open up a whole new world for yourself, internally and externally.

I know the feeling of never feeling good enough all too well. How can you know you're worthy if all you keep doing is pushing, striving and aiming higher in life, forcing your schedule to squeeze more things into your day, like a contortionist bending her body into a box?

We think we need to do more, have more and be more in order to be worthy. Then when we have what we thought we wanted, we still think we need to continue to do better and be better, in order to be worthier. We never reach the end, because we think there's always more to be done.

I also know how painful it can feel to compare yourself to others, day after day, goal after goal, achievement after achievement. It's a never-ending cycle of fear, resentment, punishment, pain and perceived 'emotional' profit. We think that if we finally reach the pinnacle of our goals, dreams and desires we'll be the happiest we've ever been; we think we can profit from the sense of achievement in ways that support us mentally, emotionally and spiritually.

But what does happen when we keep moving the goalposts, as we inevitably do? Well, I hate to break it to you, but we simply keep moving those goalposts further and further away.

There's no end to how far we can push ourselves, even though we intrinsically believe we'll never reach our goals anyway. We keep pushing on and pushing through, we keep driving ourselves into the ground, and we continue to falsely promise ourselves our idealised version of the 'promised land'—that shiny, beautiful world where self-worth is just behind every corner, where every achievement lands us a big dose of self-acceptance and external validation and recognition, and where our minds, bodies and spirits finally receive the nourishment we know they not only crave but truly, deeply deserve, even when we don't take the proper time to care for ourselves.

You may be feeling blocked by your own crushing perfectionism, by the fear that you'll never be enough or do enough or amount to anything. You may be feeling insecure about your body, your work, or any aspect of your life that you feel isn't living up to your ideal, to the potential you feel you hold so deep inside yourself.

You may not even know that you're blocking yourself from a life of clarity and confidence. You might just feel so stuck in old patterns of limiting beliefs and self-imposed rules, or beliefs and patterns passed down from your family or absorbed by close friends, that you can't see the proverbial woods for the trees.

In this book, I'll help you uncover what is blocking you from feeling worthy, confident and accepting of yourself, and why it's so important to take steps to align yourself to deep, beautiful self-care, new patterns and insights to support you on every level, as well as clear any mental, emotional and physical sabotages from your life.

Before we go on, it's important you come to your own understanding of what 'self-worth' means, as the term may not resonate with you in the same way it does with me. If that's the case, you might want to call it self-confidence, self-trust, self-love or even just understand it as a deep belief that you are good enough as you are.

All of these terms cross over with one another and yet they all mean different things to different people. Even after years in the personal development world, and even though I honour and practise this, 'self-love' is a term that doesn't always resonate with me (it kind of depends on the day!) but self-worth absolutely does.

The way I explain it to my clients is that self-worth provides a deep sense of confidence, belief, assurance and belonging in ourselves. In fact it's more than confidence—it's a deeply rooted self-belief, knowing that we are doing enough, doing the right thing, and that we don't need to earn our stripes or become more accomplished, before we think we're good enough.

I'd like to help you release that fear of never being enough. I'd like to help you feel clear when you wake up, energetically alert, awake and aligned. I'd like to help you clear the niggling negative thoughts that keep telling you that you'll only be more when you work harder; that whisper words like *You're not good enough, you'll never have what she has.* I want to help you understand what your body is trying to tell you, when you're burning out and pushing yourself to your limits in the name of self-worth, achievement and perfectionism.

I know all of this because I've lived it and because I've been able to support hundreds of women through a place of crushing self-comparison, perfectionism and low self-worth, to a place where they value, love, honour and respect themselves. It's possible for you to clear energetic, emotional, mental, physical and spiritual blocks that are making you feel anxious just reading the sentence above.

I know what you're thinking: *Sure Cass, you say that now, but there's no way I could work or push less or do less, and have more, feel more settled, more grounded, more fulfilled.* Oh, but there is. And in this book, I'll show you how.

We'll cover the reasons why you're so worried about what others think of you and how to release this, how to start living up to the best version of yourself by releasing comparison, how to start truly valuing yourself, how to adopt new mindsets that are keeping you stuck in perfectionist ways, and how to release these old attitudes. We'll look at how you can start deeply valuing and accepting yourself on all levels (yes, really!), how to recharge yourself fully and how to recognise when you're just filling your time with 'busyness' to fuel your desire to feel more worthy, and when you need to be fuelling up, instead of just filling up (and why this is so detrimental to feeling worthy and valued).

We'll also go through how to start listening to your intuition, your wisdom and higher guidance, and to your body before you burn out; how to cleanse, balance and align your physical, mental, emotional and spiritual energies (using natural remedies such as herbs, foods, movement, breath and more); and how to create your very own energetic toolkit that you can come back to again and again, so you feel swaddled in this sacred support, enabling you to give yourself permission to be the best version of yourself.

I'm excited about helping you see that you don't need to do more in order to be more, and that confidence, clarity and connection is within your reach. It's my intention that, through this book, you'll finally be able to stop striving for your self-worth, and instead start to accept, love and celebrate yourself right now. Then you can live a life that feels more connected to your potential and your purpose, where your own validation is what matters most.

ᖳ᠂ How to use this book ᠂ᖰ

I highly recommend reading this book in order, chapter by chapter, as each chapter builds on the previous one. Once you've read through it all once, feel free to come back to chapters and certain sections again and again.

Also, mind if I ask you a favour before we begin?

Please let yourself make this book 100% yours. What do I mean by that? Dog-ear the corners of pages that you love; highlight words, phrases, sentences or whole paragraphs if they ring true for you. Put hearts in the margins. (You can laugh, but I still do this when I find a paragraph I absolutely love. The heart makes it easier to find that paragraph again when I flick through the book quickly, even if that chapter is already highlighted.)

Books are sacred and your energy is sacred. So when you combine them, magic can happen. And you are so very worthy of letting magic happen for you.

So, when you're ready (and we could say you're ready now), let's make a move towards inner worthiness, empowered self-confidence and a deep sense of self-acceptance. Yes? I agree, that sounds like an excellent plan.

Part One

what's blocking you?

Chapter 1

when did we get so worried about what others think of us?

၅ပြ၅

When I think back to how much I used to worry about what others thought of me, I could shudder. I can't believe how much I allowed my perceptions of others (and often, simply my perception of **their** perception of me) to stain the way I showed up in the world, to hold me back, and to block me from being the truest version of myself.

Do you find yourself constantly worrying about what other people think of you? Perhaps you often find yourself worrying about what you **think** other people are thinking of you? Have you ever stopped to think about how this may be affecting your self-worth and your confidence, the way you show up in the world, and the way you interact with the people around you?

What needs to happen for you to finally start feeling good enough? Or will you never allow yourself that, because you don't think you're worthy of it anyway?

For us to be our best selves, we need to feel confident and comfortable enough to let go of these ties that keep us stuck and worrying about what other people think of us, to the extent that we stop showing up as our true selves. We need to trust that we are good enough as we are, notice when we're getting stuck in these energies of low self-worth and low self-confidence, and shift ourselves out of it.

Yet knowing you are worthy goes even deeper than that, because when we're being our true selves, we don't need to worry about other people, because we feel so safe with who we are. We don't need to compete with anyone (or even with ourselves), because there's no race or rush. And because we're all in this together.

I'm sure we have all felt it though; that niggling little worry that someone is staring at us, judging us, putting us down in their mind. This is not about you worrying over the clothes you're wearing, or the colour of your hair (although perhaps you're worrying about that too). Instead, I'm talking about the kind of worry that travels down into all of the layers of yourself and navigates through the deepest, darkest corners of your being. It's the kind of worry that makes you doubt yourself; from the words you speak to the way you walk, move, dress, eat and work. It's the kind of worry that makes you feel like less of a person, the kind that blocks you from feeling brave, courageous, resourceful and happy.

It's inherent in our culture, this competitive drive to be better and achieve more than we did last year, more than our friends did, more than our peers did. And even while we compete, we want to be accepted by our tribe, by our people, by our friends and family.

Even if you do think you are worthy of having more confidence, it's important to continue to truly align yourself to that confidence, and clear away any hidden cobwebs which may be holding you back on a subconscious level. Throughout this book, you'll be given the tools to do just that.

Are you feeling or noticing any of these patterns in your life?

- You constantly worry about what other people are thinking of you, and you change your essential character and behaviour to suit a perception you think someone else will prefer.
- You constantly seek external validation, because you think it's the only validation that counts.
- You often find yourself sabotaging your very best efforts when it comes to any area of your life, consciously or subconsciously.
- You're constantly comparing yourself to other people, and you never feel good enough, no matter what you do or how hard you work or how much effort you put in.
- You rarely (if ever!) give yourself a break, a rest, a reprieve, because you're worried that if you slow down or do less, you'll be even further away from feeling worthy or accepting of yourself. If you do let yourself slow down, you feel incredibly guilty and wonder if other people are judging you, while you harshly judge yourself.

❧ You know deep down you're really your worst critic and enemy, but sometimes it's easier to pretend it's not about you, and it's just that you need to work harder at gaining others' approval.

❧ You don't remember the last time you felt confident walking out of the house, at work or at a social event.

❧ You never back yourself or let yourself really receive and absorb compliments; you deflect every positive word that floats your way.

❧ You're incredibly judgemental of yourself, because you have such high expectations; except you don't think they're high, they're 'normal' to you. These high expectations slowly start to creep into other areas of your life and you find yourself judging other people or gossiping. But deep down inside you have a niggling feeling that this is all about your own insecurities and has nothing to do with anyone else.

Does any of that sound familiar? If so, you're holding the right book in your hands. If you are constantly seeking and searching for others' approval, you may be blocking yourself from listening to your inner guide, from feeling empowered and worthy, and from backing yourself and believing in yourself. Now's a really good time to let that go.

❧ A worrying waste of energy ❧

So many of us feel the need to seek and search for approval from others, and so often we succumb to feelings of low self-worth, self-confidence and self-acceptance, thinking we're not worthy of anything better.

When I was stuck in a deep sense of unworthiness, I worried about everything, all the time. I worried about whether I was eating the right thing, even when I knew my diet was healthy. I worried that I wasn't working out enough and that people were judging me at gym, because my squats weren't deep enough or I wasn't as sweaty as the girl next to me when I finished a group class. I worried if I went for coffee with a friend and she ordered a juice and I ordered a coffee. Would she judge me? Think I wasn't healthy?

When I enrolled in nutrition college, I worried that I wasn't skinny enough to be a nutritionist. I thought my peers would judge me and think I was only studying nutrition to serve my own personal needs (even though I do believe we teach what we need to learn the most—no-one learns more than the teacher). I worried that my clients wouldn't trust my advice, because of how I looked. And wow, how wrong I was!

It was **because** of everything I'd been through in my own body image journey that my clients came to me and listened to my advice. It was **because** I'd suffered from fatigue and burnout that my clients came to me and said 'yes' to the herbs I suggested. It was **because** I'd felt so unworthy and climbed out of that deep hole into somewhere much brighter and lighter that my clients came to me and allowed me to facilitate the release of trapped, stuck and heavy emotions.

What is really happening when we don't feel worthy?

Worry is a waste of energy—we've all heard that before. But how on earth can you release that worry? Where can you direct your energy instead, and how can you start believing in yourself and backing yourself so that you don't mind at all what **you think** other people think of you (or indeed, what others really do think of you)? How can you really start to believe that all that matters is that you feel secure, happy and content being exactly who you are?

I've seen this needless worrying, both in my clients and in myself. I know it can be so damaging to our psyches and incredibly draining. The good news is that we don't need to do it anymore. In fact, to continue to stay on this path of needless, draining, endless worry is one way to block yourself from truly witnessing and acknowledging how incredible you already are.

We can transmute and transform our worry. We can find a better way to funnel energy, to re-align ourselves with a higher vibration and to love the lives we're creating for ourselves. This isn't just about having blind faith or being unkind to others and thinking it doesn't matter; it's about loving and cherishing ourselves, no matter what, and letting this love and lightness vibrate out into our world and life.

I've always been someone who takes a lot of pride in my achievements. However if, through the process of reaching my goals, I didn't feel I was doing a good enough job, my perfectionism pushed me to feel as though my sense of self-worth depended on hitting self-imposed deadlines, reaching goals and achieving more and more. Sometimes this worked out in my favour, but mostly it resulted in me worrying so much about what I was or wasn't achieving, or what other people were thinking of me, that I burnt out in the process.

Have you ever heard the saying: *What someone else thinks of you is none of your business?* I remember hearing that for the first time and feeling as though a light bulb had turned on in my head. It was so true, and it was as if something in me shifted, instantly.

I had been going through a stage in my business where I felt like everything I did was being watched by my friends and peers, and I felt so judged. The truth, however, was that this judgement wasn't actually coming from anyone else—it was coming from me. Mostly, it was because I was comparing myself to everyone around me (something we'll dive into really soon). This constant comparison and criticism caused me to push myself so much harder. Yet this contracted energy was also pulling me in the direction of not accepting myself and not doing anything new or unique, because I felt that it had all been done before. I was exhausting myself.

My worry and fear about what other people were thinking didn't just affect me when it came to my work, it was also present around my body image, friendships and relationships. I always had lots of friends growing up, but I worried so much about what they thought of me. I remember getting ready to go to the beach with some friends one beautiful summer's day. I felt so nervous about being in a bikini next to my friends, as most of them were very slim. I was worried they'd judge me for not having as flat a stomach as theirs.

While I was deciding whether I should go or not, I had a realisation; I'd missed out on this exact kind of experience so many times due to low self-worth and self-confidence, and I was tired of missing out. So that day, I made myself go to the beach. I calmed my nerves by telling myself no-one would be looking at me as much as I thought, by breathing deeply and sending myself some loving compassion. I also told myself that my friends were likely as worried about their bodies as I was of mine (which isn't a lovely thought, but it took my attention away from what their perceptions of me might be).

And you know what? I went to the beach and it was beautiful. The world didn't end. No-one stared at me. We swam, chatted and laughed, we read magazines, we got fresh juices and sushi, and we had a really fun Aussie summer's day. And I would have missed that whole experience (and plenty more like it which were to come up, living in Sydney) had I let my insecurities take hold.

ᴄᴄꜱ Your sassy inner critic ꜱᴊ

Our inner judgement (camouflaged by our projections that others are judging us) causes us to push ourselves in almost every areas of our lives. If you constantly tell yourself you're not doing enough, and that you're not good enough, it's only natural your inner critic will grow in strength and sass.

There will come a time (and I sincerely hope this time is now—there's nothing like the present moment, right?) when you'll realise that the most important person who needs your approval is you. Once you realise this, take steps to affirm it and create new patterns, allowing it to be true in your life, so much can and will shift for you.

However on the flip side, if you **don't** start the work to release this exhaustive worry, whether it's just in your mind or it's showing up in all areas of your life, at some stage you will hit a wall. The wall might look pretty for a while, or it might not. Most likely, the wall will contain a doorway that opens to burnout, lowered resilience and emotional disharmony. Most likely, you'll come to realise that pushing yourself and striving for your self-worth, in order to worry less about how much you're worrying, is not going to lead you to anywhere you really want to be.

You'll slowly start to realise that pushing and striving for your self-worth isn't effective or necessary. Not only is it completely not helping you to feel more worthy, it's also exhausting and relentless. You'll realise you're expending energy on worry, and not refuelling with anything that raises your vibration and refuels your energy. There's so much going out, yet no space for anything new and vibrant to come in.

If you keep leaking energy into your worries, you'll burn out and crash. But with some awareness, it'll also likely lead you down a road that'll show you, one day, that there's so much more to life—and to yourself—than worry, perfectionism and perceptions that aren't true.

Imagine what we could do with all the energy we expend on worrying. Imagine the ideas that would flow to us, the alignments that would fall into place, the extra energy we could put towards ourselves and also those we love.

Well, ta da! Like magic, we can take that energy and shift it where we need it to be, where we want it to go.

Like magic, we can decide to tell ourselves we are good enough. We can then release worry and old perceptions and replace them with lovely, beneficial things like **confidence, clarity and courage.**

We can decide to rise above the noise our inner critic plays at full volume, and we can turn that shiz down. Right down, so low that we can't hear the din of criticism over the thrumming beat of self-confidence, the soft hum of encouragement and the smooth vibration of empowerment. We can't begin to know what others are thinking of us and, as the saying goes: *It's really none of our business anyway.* The only person who you truly need to seek approval from is yourself.

To be honest, 'seek' is the wrong word. We don't need to seek it; we need to **see** it, for it's already inside us. It always has been, it always (always!) will be.

Chapter 2

what does all this worrying accomplish?

༺༻

We grow up as part of our own little tribe of people: our family, our friends, our community at school and work. So of course, on some level, we want to attract the love, affection and attention of those around us. Yet we attract the right kind of love and attention when we are truly being ourselves, when we feel truly happy in our own lives, and when we enjoy and cultivate a deep sense of inner peace and confidence.

On the flip side, constantly worrying about what other people think is most likely making you feel even less secure and confident than you did before you began thinking like that. It might be an old pattern, and it might be because you lack the self-confidence to know and trust that things can be different. But let me tell you, they can.

I remember a time when I was in the early years of high school, feeling so insecure, wondering why I thought some people didn't want to spend time with me. One day I made the decision to 'become popular' (I know, so high school of me!) and so for weeks, I was super over-the-top friendly, I kind of sucked up to the popular girls, and I gave way more than I allowed myself to receive. Even though this persona didn't quite fit, I slowly found people were paying me more attention. It was a little bit rewarding, but it was also exhausting. It wasn't **me**. I'm not a suck-up, so all this giving, giving, giving in order to receive a non-verbal title of 'popular' was draining.

I was worrying so much about what other people were thinking of me that I was changing my entire personality to suit a mould I'd created in my imagination, a mould of the perfect little high school girl I thought other people wanted me to be.

After a while, I went back to being myself. While my popularity may have dropped a few rungs on the ladder, my cheeks stopped hurting from all my self-imposed forced smiling and I went back to being my friendly (although sometimes hard-shelled Cancerian) self.

What does all this worrying accomplish?

Apart from keeping us stuck in the mindset that we're not good enough and never will be, worrying about our self-worth achieves not much at all. Worrying about what other people think is a sure-fire way to get off track, when it comes to feeling safe and secure in your sense of self-worth. In fact, I'd go so far as to say it erodes the essence of who you are. So the more you worry, the more you erode your self-worth, and the harder it is to come back to your truest self.

The Why, What, Who of Worry

Worrying about how much you're not doing or who you're not being is not the same as clearing stress around not feeling worthy. In fact, it's likely to make you feel more unworthy and complicate things in your head, causing an overwhelmed, wishy-washy vibration.

So let's dig a little deeper. Why are you worrying? Is it just a pattern? Is there any benefit to your worrying, or is it just a perceived benefit? Does it make you feel you're being productive and getting closer to your goals or to a better outcome?

Awareness is the first step to clarity, so to support you in shifting and clearing out your worries, I have some questions for you to think about. You may want to go out and buy yourself a journal, if you don't have one already. While there aren't that many situations where you'll need to answer specific questions in this book, you may just like to have one nearby to record insights and any new awareness that drops in. Plus, it'll make up part of your Energetic Toolkit (later in the book), so you may as well get in early.

So, crack open your journal and answer these questions:

- What would happen, or what would I be able to do, if I believed in myself enough to not care so much about what others think?
- What's holding me back from doing that?
- If I could do that, how would my life feel, or what would change for me?
- Why am I so fearful of what other people think of me?

What are you worrying about?

Sometimes what we are worrying about isn't even that important to us in the long term, or it's something that'll never ever happen. Yet we continue to worry about how we'll deal with it if it does.

Here are some questions to ask yourself:

- What am I really worried about?
- Why does this matter to me so much?
- What's the likelihood of my worry coming true? And if it does come true, what's the worst thing I'm imagining that could happen? And if the worst thing that I'm imagining actually happened, what would I do? How would I manage it?
- How else can I approach this situation, without overwhelming myself with worry, and without needing the approval of others?

✿ Who are you worrying about? ✿

This is a big question. When you worry about what other people are thinking of you, who is your main focus? Why are you zeroing in on them? Is it because you admire them? Do you look up to them and wish they paid you more attention? Perhaps they intimidate you and make you feel nervous or perhaps you just really enjoy being around them, and want to become closer to them.

Here are some questions to ask yourself:

- Who is my 'worry focus' on?
- Why am I focusing on this person so much? What's this indicating to me? For example, do I admire them and want to become closer to them? Am I intimidated by them, yet want their support or friendship? Do I want them to like me?
- What can I to do to feel more comfortable about this situation, or in this person's presence?
- How can I release my worries about this person?

Caring so much about what other people think of you might be something you grew up with. Perhaps it's a family pattern, where there has always been a lot of focus on external approval and worrying about what others think of you. Perhaps it's just part of your culture or friendship circle. Maybe the only way you feel you can 'get ahead' is by ensuring everyone else approves of you, before you approve of yourself.

This may work for you for a little while, but it won't last forever. Your sense of self-worth needs to be kept sacred and nourished; running on others' self-approval as your energy source is not sustainable. You can only renew your own energy, not someone else's.

Unless you're incorporating practices into your everyday life which infuse your body, mind and spirit with energy, confidence and remembering your worth, you may continue on this cycle of never feeling good enough, and constantly worrying about what others are thinking of you.

Chapter 3

working with your flow

෩

If you are to release the pattern of worrying about what other people think of you, and instead start grounding yourself in your true potential, then it's crucial you adopt some empowered mindset shifts. This will help you to instil a deep sense of self-belief into everything you do.

The whole premise of negative mindset patterns is in the title—they're a pattern. They've been wired in your mind to repeat and repeat and repeat. I want to help you break that loop, and rewire your mind to a lighter, empowered way of thinking. If you can just start, you can keep going.

✌ Things need to change ✍

There are four mindset shifts that can benefit us when it comes to releasing our perception ('perception' being the most important word) of what other people think of us, or our perception of how we're showing up in the world, in order to fully feel our worth as human beings, without having to do more, be more, have more or prove ourselves to anyone.

I call it **FLOW**:

1. Follow your own path
2. Let go of your perceptions
3. Open up to new attitudes and patterns
4. Work with what you have

Working with the FLOW approach allows you to clear some of the sabotages that run through your mind on repeat, and cause you to keep worrying about what other people are (most likely not) thinking about you.

Let's go through them now. As you read, I want you to try and place yourself in the energy of this new approach, and think of personal experiences that you could learn from. Keep your journal nearby to record new intentions and insights.

Follow your own path

Sometimes we worry about taking our own steps forward and forging our own path, because of the paths others have taken before us. This could be something that's been passed down in your family. Maybe your father was an accountant, and his father was an accountant, and his father's father was a accountant. So when you say you want to study art, chaos and judgement follows.

While we can't always change what other people are thinking of us, we can release our fear around not meeting their expectations when we decide to take our own path.

Following your own path might not make sense to anyone else, and that's okay. The more you feel centred in your decision, the more aligned you can be about clarifying your vision and purpose. Then the easier it will be to stay on your path, whether you think it'll make someone else happy or not.

Let go of your perceptions

Your perceptions are simply perceptions; they're your ego's way of keeping you exactly where you are, because that's where it feels safest. You can let go of your perceptions, you can let go of your worry. Let your worry fuel your desire to let it all go. Your perceptions of how other people perceive you can be tainted by your ego, but also often by a lack of communication. When you can fully let go of these perceptions, you'll find it so much easier to stop worrying about what other people think of you.

There's no magic formula for doing this. In the past, the best thing I could do for myself when I knew I was worrying too much about others' opinions was to strengthen my sense of self-esteem, self-worth and self-confidence; all of which you'll be learning how to do in this book.

ﻉﻉ Open up to new attitudes and patterns ﻝﻝ

Much like letting go of your perceptions, sometimes just opening up the lines of communication with others, creating new patterns and creating space for these new patterns to enter your mind and your life is an important first step.

When I was in high school, the principal once told my parents that I used to look quite mean when I walked around school (you may have jokingly heard the term 'Resting Bitch Face'! Would now be a good time to tell you my hubby sometimes teasingly calls me RBF?) but that when I smiled, it warmed my whole face and energy.

His perception was that I wasn't happy until I smiled, but actually, sometimes I just look like that when I'm not smiling. Imagine if he'd never seen me smile, he may have just thought I was always unhappy! He had a perception that I didn't like him (even though he was the coolest principal ever—and no, those aren't words one usually utters) yet as soon as he voiced this, he understood that it was just his perception.

A new attitude might mean that you spend time working out what your triggers are as well. What makes you think someone else doesn't like you? What makes you worry that someone is unhappy with you or your work? Is it just a fleeting expression on their face? Could you have mistaken that look for contempt, when maybe they just realised their shirts are still at the drycleaners and now it's too late to pick them up?

Your perceptions and your attitudes are so linked. It's important to work out when you're being blocked or blocking yourself, so you can create healthier new patterns, and then give yourself permission to simply let it go.

Work with what you have

A lot of our worry about what other people are thinking of us comes down to self-esteem, self-belief and self-worth. This can relate to your solar plexus chakra energy, which I'll discuss with you further along in this book.

How many times have you thought to yourself, *I think she'd like me more if I were more XYZ* or *He's definitely unimpressed with me because I don't have enough XYZ?* Now, this thing you have or don't have could be something personal or emotional, or a physical product or item. The truth is, we're always given what we can handle and manage. So if you don't have this 'thing', you most likely really don't need it (now or ever).

Instead of making yourself believe that you'll be better or more liked or more popular if you have more (of anything!), I want you to start believing that you have everything you need right now. And if you needed more, you'd have it. Work with what you have, realising that all the good stuff you still want is in your reach, but it won't make you a better person all on its own. You'll make yourself a better person, starting right now. It won't make you change your perceptions or attitudes. Only you can do that.

Now that you understand a little more of what's underneath you worrying about what other people think of you, let's move into the next chapter and help you clear some of the emotional conflict that comes up when you constantly compare yourself to other people.

Chapter 4

an infatuation with comparison

⚬⚬⚬

A client of mine once told me a story about how she would constantly compare herself to a colleague in her office, to the point where she could barely speak to her during meetings, so strong was her envy. She consciously knew that she was slightly obsessed with comparing herself to this person, and deeply wanted to release these thoughts. At the same time, she was hating and berating herself for doing it, and complaining about it to her close friends.

I used to be infatuated with comparing myself to other people in my industry too. It was simultaneously painful and annoying to watch myself doing it, yet frustratingly, like scratching a mosquito bite or playing with a loose tooth, it felt good in some way and I couldn't stop. All I could tell myself was that I wasn't good enough, and that I'd never

have or 'get to' where they were, and I kept scratching that
itchy bite until it bled.

I found myself in a pattern. I'd zero in on one person and
compare myself to every aspect of their work, their website,
their achievements, and even the glimpses of their life that
I'd see on social media (sometimes I'd even compare my
body to their bodies and their looks). I'd do this until I was
blue in the face, until I couldn't write my own blog posts or
find my own voice, until I felt like an absolute failure and
wondered why I was even trying to create my own business,
when they clearly had something much better than I could
ever create and this clearly meant I couldn't have it too.
Drama queen, much?

I compared myself to people who were my peers, my equals
and my friends. Even if I felt close to some of these people,
even if I truly admired their work and applauded them, all
I could see (or thought I could see, with my 'comparison
blinkers' on) was that I wasn't enough. Not today, not this
week, not ever. I didn't allow myself to lean into my own
potential, because I was so incredibly focused on theirs.

Once I'd exhausted all possible avenues of comparison
for one person, and made myself feel incredibly insecure, I'd
move on to someone else. Each time I did this , I lowered my
sense of self-worth and heightened my emotional sensitivity,
continuing to find ways to drag myself through the mud from
my lack of self-worth. I deepened the hole I was digging
for myself because, while I was looking at everyone else,

I couldn't look to myself to find the ladder I needed to simply climb out of it.

I knew on some level there was something I had to shift. But I felt really lost and stuck as to exactly what it was or how to go about doing it … until there came a time when I decided enough was enough. I knew I was sabotaging myself on every level. I knew I wasn't allowing true growth, fulfil-ment or satisfaction to enter my life because, in truth, I was actually becoming obsessed with not being good enough.

'Obsessed' is a strong word, but in reality it makes sense. Everything we feel when we're comparing ourselves to others feels intense. We exaggerate what we're feeling because, while we're feeling it, we wonder how we'd ever let it go; we moan and complain about how much we're lacking or how much we don't understand why someone else has something we want. We say unkind things to others out of jealousy or envy. We want to be happy for others, but we also want to look after ourselves. We procrastinate out of fear, perfectionism and self-sabotage, because putting things on hold and blocking ourselves to getting where we want to be before we give ourselves the chance to get there is an easy way to tell ourselves we've done something productive, something helpful, something that will support us.

It's instant gratification at it's finest. The things we see others having may have taken them a decade to create for themselves and we want it **now**. And if we can't have it because they've already got it, or because we can't see how the future will pan out for us, it's easier to simply wipe our hands and get back to our lack mentality.

Thinking you're not good enough is sometimes easier than owning your worth. It takes courage to stand up and start trusting yourself, to tell yourself you're worthy and truly believe it. It takes effort and a deep commitment to love yourself, to be compassionate, and to be okay with being human—guilt, shame, fear and all. It takes strength and awareness to be able to discern when your inner critic is just saying things to keep you safe, to keep you exactly where you are, and to stop you from taking risks that could mean you end up really living your purpose. And our inner critic is **always** saying things to keep us safe; it's got our back, but it's on the wrong side of personal success and growth. It thinks we'll be more successful if we don't leap, if we don't speak up, if we don't do things we've never done before. It keeps us rooted in fear, the kind of fear that makes playing small seem easier, better, safer and more reasonable.

But constantly playing small, staying safe and being reasonable isn't why we're here. We don't need to follow the status quo, because the status quo was created by those who followed their inner critic's fear and said 'no' when they may have been better off saying 'yes' or 'why' or 'no thanks, I'll have better than that, I am better than that.'

I realised how tired I was of comparing myself to everyone else, so I made a commitment: I vowed to stop comparing myself to others, and to finally feel into my powerful self.

I knew she was in there and I knew the time was ripe to coax her out. I worked out how to shift and release all the stuff that was holding me prisoner in my own energetic prison; how to use it or lose it; how to live up to the very best version of me, today. So now I'm buzzing to show you how I did this, and help you bring more awareness to your own comparison challenges, so you can release them once and for all too.

Why are we obsessed with comparing ourselves to other people?

I don't think we mean to be obsessed, but sometimes it's easier to compare ourselves than to look at our own lives and take action on our dreams.

Working through my own comparison limitations and helping my clients work through theirs, I've found there seems to be six ways we use comparison to block ourselves, to berate ourselves, to disaffirm our happiness and to keep us stuck in the spiteful cycle of comparison and self-sabotage.

As you read through the rest of this chapter, I suggest you be aware of who you're comparing yourself to (although you're not likely to forget, right?); what it is that you're really wanting e.g. what this comparison is saying to you; and what may be triggering you to feel worse, e.g. spending time on social media, thinking negative thoughts about the other person or yourself, or procrastinating on creating your own waves of change in your life.

At the end of Chapter 6, this you'll find a worksheet to help release comparison. It will include some of these questions, but it's good to start bringing awareness to these underlying issues and energies now.

☙ Comparison Block #1 ❧

You compare yourself to your 'perfect' self

This is the 'you' you wish you could be, if only you were absolutely perfect and did everything the way you think you **should** be doing it, never felt scared, always knew what was around the corner, and always had the upper hand in every situation. You constantly wish you were further along your current path and berate yourself for being where you are, who you are and not as perfect as you think you should be. You constantly have thoughts of *Oh, if only I were more … or had more of … or knew more about …*

You are your own worst critic; always thinking you could do better, should do better and would do better if things were different for you in some way. On bad days you feel slightly victimised and on good days, when things do go perfectly to plan, you use that as fuel to fire yourself up and stay on your perfectionist path.

You have very little compassion for yourself and always push yourself to do more. This comparison causes you to never be truly happy with where you are, because you never feel you reach your version of your perfect self. So how on earth could you be happy and appreciative of where you are? You feel there's still so much work to be done, and you're the first (and sometimes the only one) to admit it.

⟨ Comparison Block #2 ⟩

You compare yourself to your ideal potential

Your version of yourself as this 'ideal potential' is even further along your path and more enigmatic than your perfect self. You degrade your visions of your dreams and goals because you don't feel worthy of having them anyway, so why should you dream now? You think that if you were more perfect, everything would fall into place like Cinderella's glass slipper, as the prince slipped it on her perfect foot.

You don't feel you'll ever reach the version of yourself that you desire, mostly because you have zero patience. You 'future trip' and live in the future, never really committing to anything now, or sabotage your best efforts at creating your potential because it seems so far away and you don't think it's possible for you anyway. You just really aren't happy and have no idea how to move forwards.

Future tripping keeps you planted firmly where you are, because you're looking so far ahead you can't take one small step in front of the other, because that means looking down at where you are for just a moment, and that's terrifying.

✧ Comparison Block #3 ✧

You compare yourself to your past

Perhaps you feel you've declined in a certain area of your life, so you're always trying to get back to where you used to be, or reach a goal you once reached. This kind of comparison also keeps you pretty stuck; part of you desperately wants to move forwards, but the other part is worried that the further you move ahead, the less likely you are to get back to where you've been in the past.

You sabotage yourself by listening to your inner critic who says you're past your prime; you'll never be as thin, healthy, wealthy, recognised or accomplished as you used to be, so what's the point in trying? Trying is new, different, uncertain and, since you have no assurance that things will go back to how they once were, you have no real desire to attempt to create something (anything!) that could be even more unique and incredible for yourself. Something that matches who you are **now**, as opposed to your 'perfect' past self.

✧ Comparison Block #4 ✧

You compare yourself to other people

This one needs little explanation. It's the most obvious form of comparison, and the most common that I see in my clients and indeed in myself. Obvious in that you might get a familiar twinge every time you do it, and common because you may find yourself comparing yourself to another person every day in some form.

ᴄᴇᴊ Comparison Block #5 ᴄᴊᴊ

You compare yourself to others' potential

In this mindset, you expend too much energy thinking about other peoples' future work and accomplishments, stuff that hasn't even happened! You wonder what they'll do next, and tell yourself it'll be better than anything you could ever do, which of course ensures you feel this way. This is where you place people on pedestals and completely disillusion yourself with a made-up version of a reality that doesn't even exist yet.

ᴄᴇᴊ Comparison Block #6 ᴄᴊᴊ

You compare yourself to people who are years ahead of you

There's another little block that I found myself going through which really could be a part of Block #5, as it ties in so much to living out our potential.

Stuck in this mindset block, you compare yourself to others who **are** living out their potential; they are living their lives with passion, drive and commitment. They show up every day, they take risks and don't get attached to the outcome. They feel fear but instead of shying away, they allow themselves to fully feel it and not run away from it.

For me, this block was another hurdle I had to leap over, and it was a hard pill to swallow. Although not as persistent as the some of the other stages or blocks of comparison that I went through, it could have been one of the most damaging for me, had I let myself soak in it.

I had just graduated as a nutritionist and started seeing clients, and found myself looking up to several well-established naturopaths. Many of these women had been working for years; in fact, one of the naturopaths to whom I compared myself had been working for almost two decades. Of course she knew more than I did and had a well-established business; she'd been working at it since I was eight years old!

I remember feeling so low and panicky when I'd think about how far ahead of me she was. At the time, I thought I wanted the business model she had, and I wanted it **now**. I came home and spoke to my husband about it, feeling quite stressed out. My husband repeatedly tried to soothe my stresses by reminding me that I'd been working for only several months, and this woman had been working for almost two decades.

I thought I'd never know as much as she knew, or have as many clients as she did, or understand herbal medicines the way she did. Apart from making me feel like a failure (which I wasn't), all this stressing and comparison made me feel like nothing I did was good enough (when it was), and that nothing was helping me move forwards. When I think back to that time, all I want to say to myself is, 'Calm yourself, Cass'.

Even while I stressed myself out over this, I knew the truth: she was older and more experienced, yet she had started out exactly as I had. I didn't actually aspire to create a business like hers or follow her business model at all. I had to fully feel everything I needed to feel, to realise my own truth. Yes, I loved seeing clients and making beautiful herbal medicine formulas for them, but I didn't want to manage stock in a big store or clinic, or manage other people.

Finding my truth under my pain was an incredible relief. I would build up my own business, my own body of knowledge, my own dreams. And I could do it when I let go of trying to carry someone else's.

A work in progress is the best kind of progress

If these stories and insights sing out to you and made you nod, cry or laugh in recognition, then we're onto a good thing here, and that makes me happy.

Comparison is part of the human condition. We are hardwired to look to others in our tribe to see what they're up to, but we don't have to let it condition us to believe we're less worthy.

Coming up, I'll offer you some sweet tools to help you start facing your comparison blocks and work to shift and release them; let go of your fear that you're not good enough and never will be; and offer some insights into how you can ensure you know deep down in your belly that your work-in-progress self is truly the best version of yourself, already.

Chapter 5

what can comparison cause and create?

 barrison can create so much strife and pain in our lives if we hold onto it or don't transmute and transform its powerful energy into something that can enliven and awaken us to our true potential.

It keeps us feeling separate from those around us, and especially from those to whom we compare ourselves. When we feel separate, as though we don't belong, our choices don't always reflect our highest selves. The energy of constant comparison ensures we think we're different from others, and not made of the right stuff. When we feel less worthy than others, we energetically put up barriers and block ourselves from receiving what we need, what we desire and what we want to manifest—the things that would help us put this all into perspective and come out brighter and lighter on the other side. Things like insight into what's triggering us to feel this way; a rational perspective; the compassion to self-soothe ourselves and take our hands off the proverbial flame; and the drive, desire and commitment to create our own bricks, so we can pave our own way.

When we compare ourselves to others, we find ourselves full of guilt, doubt, shame, uncertainty and fear. It creeps in and, like a vapour, it touches everything in our lives yet we can't always see it. And if we don't locate or create the resources and use our inner resourcefulness to release it, we allow this stuff to stay stuck. It's stuff we don't truly need, yet letting it go feels dangerous, difficult sometimes. We make up stories in our head about why other people are doing better than we are, about why we'll never have what they have, and, of course, we agree when we tell ourselves that we're not good enough to have it anyway, so why bother?

We compare ourselves to other people for so many reasons, sometimes to such a degree that we're completely blind to the effects this is having on us—on our relationships, our self-confidence and our self-esteem, even on our progress and path in life.

To help you shift gears on this, let's take a look now at what comparison can cause and create in our minds, bodies, spirits and lives.

Comparison lowers our self-worth and self-confidence

We get stuck in a lower vibration, and it's from this vibration that we're more likely to act out of fear and self-preservation (which isn't always the same as self-improvement and progression). It's not because we're scared and selfish, it's because we've disempowered ourselves and the unknown feels terrifying. We fear taking a risk and leaping, because we can't even see a corner of this net people always talk about.

We believe that what we have isn't good enough and that, because someone else has it, we'll never be able to have it too. From this lower vibration it's much harder to align ourselves to our own worth and confidence and show up in our own lives.

Comparison blocks our energy and alignment

When we're in a state of comparison, we're blind to our own genius, our own accomplishments, our own beauty, the abundance that's around us and to the incredible parts of our lives that usually make us happy. We feel drained and exhausted by the prospect of having to work so much harder than we currently do, in order to have what we want (or feel we deserve). So we fall out of alignment with our true selves and our higher vision.

Comparison cripples our creativity and limits our voice

The more we look at others' work, the less we can see our own. The more we try to create what someone has already created, the further away we feel from creating what we're supposed to be creating.

We stop being productive and we lose focus; we waste hours putting energy into thoughts that leave us spiralling down a long staircase into the depths of despair. And all because we're operating from a lack mentality.

In the middle of my comparison, I felt paralysed and stuck for weeks, comparing my unfinished work with the work of my mentors, peers and friends. I knew this had to end, or I'd never make any progress in my life, and my life's work. Instead of the comparison acting like fuel in a positive way, it meant I couldn't do the work I was here to do.

I remember that during the process of writing my first ebook, I stopped about halfway through. I quite literally didn't know how to write using my own voice, with my own vision and my own touch. I had to take a very big step back and cut the cords to my comparison; I didn't want it controlling me anymore.

Your voice can't sound like anyone else's because it doesn't need to. It need only sound like yours. The challenge here isn't in how to copy someone else while making it still sound like you; it's in how to coax yourself out and trust what you find. You'll only know what your voice sounds like when you're brave enough to use it.

ୡୠ Comparison creates drama ୶ୢ

Wherever I compared myself to others, I also seemed to dramatise everything. Nothing felt good enough and yet everything felt like a huge deal. I don't usually attract drama into my life, yet I've never felt as close to drama and creating mountains out of molehills as I did in those months of deep comparison and undervaluing myself.

Even though comparison came from a place of low self-worth, it seemed to make me feel like an even lesser version of myself. I found myself having to bite my tongue when certain people would come up in conversation, because my insecurity meant it was hard for me to send them love and praise their work. (When I'm feeling 'myself', this is something that's very easy for me to do.)

You might have friends who attract or create drama, yet comparison doesn't seem to be a major player in their lives (though perhaps low self-worth is). But take notice now if you're creating drama, if you're making spectacles of your friends' successes and finding it hard to be genuinely happy for other people, sensationalising how you're feeling or bitching about others and their achievements, because their success is hard for you to swallow.

You're not a bad person for feeling this way or saying unkind things, even about those you admire; you're feeling this way because, on some level (conscious or not), you feel insecure about your own achievements (which I'm sure are perfectly perfect for you at this exact moment in time).

Make the commitment to drop the drama and cease all nasty remarks about others. Instead, help others rise, raise the collective vibration, and follow your intuition about where to invest your energy. It's surely guiding you as far away from the theatre as possible.

Comparison makes us rush ahead

Sometimes comparison is a way of rushing ahead, not staying in the present moment and not having full trust in the path that lies before you. We want to skip steps and race to the finish line, forgetting that every small step counts, forgetting that there is no finish line.

I would often feel so content and happy being on my own path … until I saw someone else's path. Gah! That's when the feelings of low self-worth would creep back in, leading me off my path as I searched to find the way onto someone else's.

Comparison creates a sense of lack (and keeps us stuck there)

When we're comparing, we feel like we could never have what other people have. They already have it, so what's left for us? We feel jealous, envious and small. We feel frustrated and resentful, because we feel that we've worked so hard too, so why don't we have what they have?

We believe there isn't enough for us, so we create this as our reality. We hear about people and friends who have so much so we believe that, like the old tale of how the animals got their coats, there's nothing left for us but the wrinkly old elephant skin (which in itself is beautiful, right?).

What we believe in this mindset is what we then go on to create for ourselves, as hard as that pill is to swallow. If we feel small, we act small. So when we feel small and defeated we must be brave enough to release ourselves from the pull of lack, scarcity and feeling like we have to compete with those around us, or those we've put on pedestals. There is no pedestal but the one you've created in your mind, so you're the only one who can pull it down and put it away. You're the one who can create more in your life, you're the one who can open your heart, your mind, your energy and say, 'I'm ready for more, I know there's (more than) enough for me and I'm making space for it to come to me, in whatever form is best. I know I'm so very worthy of it. Bring it on!'

✎ Comparison creates a victim mentality ✐

Following on from feeling stuck in a sense of lack, when we're deep in the comparison cave we may even feel victimised.

People who victimise themselves are so stuck in fear, lack and a blame mentality that they 'cut off their nose to spite their face' on a daily basis. They don't take action when they could, because they feel the risks are too great. Let me be brutally (but lovingly!) honest … people who play the victim may even say they have a deep sense of self-awareness, but they're blinded by their procrastinating, fearful ego.

They find themselves incredibly resentful of the success of others, putting it down to luck, family wealth or something else they couldn't possibly create for themselves, because that is so much easier than actually working hard for something, or learning a new skill, or creating a healthier mindset or releasing worries and leaning into their fear. Their ego takes over their insular world where they feel safe, while simultaneously blaming something outside of themselves for their lack of success, external validation or acknowledgement.

There is no sense of urgency in their lives because their ego tells them that even if they tried harder, they can't have what someone else has. They've been taken over by their inner critic and until they turn the volume down on that voice, they're bound to stay stuck for good.

Comparison confuses us

We latch on to certain ideas about what we want or what we think we should want, without ever asking ourselves if we truly want to be heading in that direction.

Honestly, sometimes after a little introspection you might even come to realise you don't want the things you thought you wanted, or that they're just not possible for you in this lifetime (like that time I wished I had an older brother or a twin sister; sorry, not gonna happen Cass); be it the house your friends just bought (but you've got extra cash for that long-awaited trip to Europe now); the promotion (but actually, your free time and blissful weekends are looking pretty sweet right about now); or the new relationship (if you think about it, you're really happy where you are, being solo for a little bit). It's highly possible you're actually pretty happy with where you are, and who you are, right now.

When it comes down to it, and when you can really look at your life without putting yourself down about where you're **not**, you'll see you have so much. Think about what it is you're truly desiring and then ask yourself: *Do I have the means to manage this right now? Do I have the systems, the support or the time for this right now? What would happen if I snapped my fingers and could have this? Is it what I really want?*

Your answer may surprise you. You'll see that you can have a different kind of freedom and joy … one that is purely yours. As soon as you realise this, you'll be able to relax into your current situation and current self, and be profoundly grateful for all you do have, and even for what you don't have (yet … or ever).

We can call this being grateful, being honest with what we truly want, being happy with where we are in life, and trusting that we'll be further along our path when we're ready to be there. We're never given more than we can manage, so if you don't have what you want yet, it could just mean you don't have what you want … yet.

Comparison keeps us stagnant

In my comparison days, it was as if I were walking around in a negative, dreary, dark fog of my own creation. Only I could see the fog, and only I could lift it.

Sometimes we worry so much about whether or not we'll ever have what someone else has, that we stop ourselves from creating our own way forward, from taking those first few steps down our own track, the one that allows us to reach our **own** version of this.

Imagine now there was a way to shift these feelings, emotions, patterns and mindsets? Imagine someone could swoop in and take this pain away, putting the energy to better use?

Ah, but there is, and it's already inside you, silly. Your inner ally is just waiting to be given permission to pop up from underneath disempowerment and the lack mentality of: *I never have enough, there's never enough for me; someone else already has it.*

Shall we go find the key to the doorway into the true abundance, confidence and worth that is already yours? (This is when you say, 'Yes, Cass!')

Chapter 6

coaxing out your inner ally

❧

After months of my internal critic going berserk at me daily (so freaking exhausting!) I knew something had to change. So one day, after months of internal criticism and comparison, my inner ally (who, it turns out, is actually an absolute hero in the quest to quieten my inner critic) finally spoke up, loud and clear saying:

> *Stop this, Cass. You don't have to be better than anyone else, you just have to be the very best version of who you are. If you could just let go of this comparison and nastiness, you'd see the best version of you is already staring back at you in the mirror. Also, that's actually a really nice mirror, where's it from …?*

You have an inner ally too, and it's time to coax this powerful player out.

Through a little more digging, a little more awareness and a lot of letting go, you'll be able to adopt a few simple mindset shifts and embrace a few simple changes to your daily routine (and thought patterns), which will support you in getting out of the comparison trap you've set for yourself.

To begin, please ask yourself these questions (clarity is a lovely little thing):

🔖 Do I even want to be comparing myself?
🔖 Am I comparing myself for any apparent benefit?
🔖 Is the thing I'm comparing myself to something that I really want? … or
🔖 Is this just a bad habit, a habit I've formed to protect me from doing the work to attain the things I truly want?

Here are some things you might like to try to help coax out your inner ally. All of these suggestions are things I've done myself. They really helped my inner ally come out of hiding and feel comfortable enough to stay, for good.

❧ Know there's enough for you ☙

Before we go one step further I have to tell you something really important. It's so important that I need you to really believe me when I say it, because believing this is one of the most important things you can do for yourself on this journey of knowing your worth and getting out of the comparison trap.

So here we go. Ready?

There is enough for you. Take that in for a moment. I know! Sounds crazy, right? How can there be enough for me **and** you? How can there be enough money, success, love, happiness, clients, work and abundance?

There is enough. In fact, there's more than enough. But when we're stuck comparing ourselves to others and feeling **less than**, we can't see how much there is for us. We miss opportunities and chances to truly receive abundance, and we rush past signs and guidance which could be really supportive for us.

Ultimately, making friends with envy and releasing comparison comes down to knowing there is enough for you. It's about knowing how you really **want** to feel, not how you think you **should** feel, then taking action to feel that way.

On a deeper level, this means knowing you are enough. It means knowing you are worthy. It means knowing there is space for you to have what you want. It means asking tough questions such as:

- What is my comparison trying to show me?
- Where is it guiding me?
- What's the lesson in my pain?
- How can I make this work for me?
- How can I take action to create what I want and open up to receive what I desire?

It means knowing that when you see something in someone else that you want, it's only triggering these feelings in you because it's saying you can have this too. What will help you get there is courage. I have a post-it on my desk with a quote from best-selling author Brené Brown, who says, *You can have courage and comfort, but you can't have both.*

Knowing there's enough for you is about being brave enough to step up, lean into your uncertainty, let go of the pain and understand your triggers, so you can work out what your version of a golden life (and that's **your** golden life, your most beautifully perfect, imperfect life) can look like, and then taking inspired action to make it happen.

And yes, sometimes your jealousy, envy or resentment shouts and screams at you until you listen to it. Sometimes it's a very painful lesson, and it's repeated over and over again until you're sure there's not much left of you to hurt. But it's simply a lesson.

And while it's certainly not the end of the world, it could spell the beginning of another beautiful, perfectly imperfect chapter of your life. So learn from it, grow from it, and find your own sense of deep emotional harmony because of it.

Do the opposite

Know that it's okay to do the opposite of what your nasty, obsessive compulsive, perfectionist inner critic tells you to do. If your inner critic is saying, *OMG please stay on this website*

and stab your eyeballs out with jealousy and envy and lack.
*Read about all the things you're **not** doing and make yourself*
feel small and insignificant because, duh, you are, then I give
you full permission to close your laptop and back away from
the computer.

Bend and breathe and flow it out

I always tell my clients there'll never be just **one** thing that
changes everything for you. It'll always be a combination of
mindset shifts, insights, healings, modalities and changes
that you implement. However, I feel it would be remiss of
me if I didn't say that yoga was one of the most important
things I started doing for myself (and continue to do). Yoga
helped me find my flow again, align my energy and get out
of the comparison trap.

When I would get stuck in the zone of comparison, one
of the best things I could do was step away from my laptop
or shut off the social media channels I was surfing and get
my sorry-for-myself mind and body to a yoga class.

Yoga continues to be a source of flow, ease and joy for
me. In fact, as I write this, I've just left a blissful 6am yoga
class. This particular class is taught by one of my favourite
yoga teachers. She is a favourite because she doesn't take
life too seriously and makes the entire class laugh with her
simultaneous lightness, seriousness and heartfelt clarity of
thought, while she trips over the corner of a yoga mat and
laughs at herself (ah, sweet, sweet lightness). Today's theme

was 'surrender, the art of powerful non-resistance', which is what letting go of comparison is all about. Non-resistance, surrender, movement, letting go and going with the flow.

&c; Don't be drained &cp;

Comparison can drain you on every level and, if the comparison doesn't, the ensuing drive of over-commitment to push yourself to exhaustion so you can prove yourself will.

For this reason, ensuring you keep your energy protected and balanced is important. This may mean spending less time with certain people who you feel trigger something in you that leaves you feeling flat, low or fragile. This doesn't have to be forever, just until you regain some confidence and create healthy energetic boundaries, which we'll discuss later on.

Start to see your energy as a renewable resource. It can be renewed and replenished when you set the intention to do so, create the space to follow through and then follow your heart on what you need to do.

&c; Stop following the apple of your inner critic's eye &cp;

I've given this advice to many of my clients and in online courses I've taught, and I've had such a wonderful response. For me, being on social media and being bombarded with images and updates from the people I was comparing myself to was like rubbing salt into my wounds. I needed to cut that out of my life for a little while and let my wounds heal. (And yes, I really did feel 'wounded'.)

Giving yourself space from people you are comparing yourself to can be really refreshing thing. When I did this, my comparison dropped from a self-rated 110% down to 20–30%, just through this action alone. The less I saw, the less I put myself down while I was building myself back up again.

Doing this doesn't mean you don't respect and admire these people, or that you aren't inspired or awed by them, it just means you know you have to put yourself first (without feeling guilty about it), to give yourself time to build your confidence and self-belief up. (Which is awesome, and you can be proud of yourself for doing so.)

⟨⟨ Reduce your scroll time ⟩⟩

Even if I wasn't looking at a particular person's website or social media account, I also stopped scrolling through news feeds for a while. (So much time, energy and creativity is wasted by scrolling through news feeds.)

In fact, I reduced my screen time in general, unless I was sitting down to do my own work. I don't actually read a lot of blogs or online news, but I stopped clicking through links and spending a lot of time online, on news sites and on other peoples' websites. I just found it used up so much of my energy and left me feeling really drained and flat. Before I had fully dealt with my comparison issues, when I was online I would inevitably come across websites, people, articles and images that kept me trapped in the comparison vortex. I knew this wasn't helping my situation; I knew that while I was in this super fragile place, the best thing for me to do was spend less time online, and more time in the real-life, tangible world.

So this is what I used to do: I'd log into my social media accounts to post my own work and insights, check and reply to comments and then log off. Sometimes I'd click over to my friends' accounts and give them some online love (a 'Like' or 'Share' here or there) but that was it.

Instead of scrolling through the feeds, where can you funnel that energy? How much better might you feel if you energetically put up a few more boundaries, keeping your energy close to where you need it most right now—your heart?

When I would get offline and into my life, spending time with the people I love, the animals I love (fluffy dog cuddles are the best thing ever), drinking the teas I love (is anyone else obsessed with licorice and peppermint tea?), doing things I love like reading, watching movies, hanging out in cafes and at yoga, going to the beach and the park, then I would find myself coming back to my true self. My true self can see what others are doing and respect it, without dragging myself or anyone else down in the process.

⟡ Extend love ⟡

When it felt like the comparison was getting too much to bear, I sat down at my computer and sent off a little love note:

Dear [Name], I just wanted to let you know that I think you're absolutely wonderful. Your work is amazing and inspires me no end, your website is beautiful, and I adore your weekly emails. Thank you so much for putting yourself out there every single day. Gratefully, Cassie.

I didn't expect a thing in return. Just pressing 'send' gave me such instant gratification. I felt a huge lightness wash over me. I **almost instantly** stopped comparing myself to this person. It was incredible!

And guess what? I did receive a lovely reply. Just making a connection with the real-life human on the other end of my envy brought me back down to real life and allowed me to focus on my own path again.

I realised this person was just like me, waking up every day and hoping they were doing the right thing, investing their energy where it felt right, and trying to show up in the world as best they could. For the first time in a long time, I could take a deep breath … in and out … and feel so much more like myself.

Since then, if ever I find myself in the position where I'm comparing myself to other people, I send a little love note (be it electronic or via snail mail). I have even sent gorgeous little gift packs of notebooks, pens and beautiful stationery to people I admire and feel inspired by. I love giving presents, and giving something out that you know might make someone's day, with no expectation of anything in return, is a wonderful thing.

ᴄᴇ Send some more love (to yourself) ᴊ

Compassion, compassion, compassion! I can almost guarantee you are being more than a little unkind to yourself, when you constantly compare yourself to other people. Am I right?

Sending yourself a little love and compassion can be as simple as taking time out to do something that leaves you feeling centred, grounded and whole: taking yourself off to a weekend retreat somewhere in the forest or near a beach; or booking a massage or a girls' night out; or absolutely anything that takes your fancy.

It can also just mean taking the pedal off the metal and giving yourself time to nourish, nurture, rest and restore yourself. Are you pushing yourself way too hard? When was the last time you **really** took a break? No, not that break. You felt guilty then, didn't you? I mean, when was the last time you really took a break and felt amazing for taking it?

If the idea of taking a break leaves you with sweaty palms, the naturopath in me says that's a sign of adrenal depletion and an overactive nervous system, and the kinesiologist in me wants to help you clear the guilt and worry you feel around resting and taking care of yourself. All of that (and more!) is coming up later in the book.

ᴄᴇ Dig a little deeper and find your triggers ᴊ

It's important you start to discover what (or who) these triggers may be, especially if you're feeling a little emotionally fragile. Start to get a feel for what your body is saying to you by listening to its cues. This change in your awareness will be really helpful in aligning yourself to the people, practices and energy you want to be connected to.

What are your triggers? By that I mean, what makes you feel worse when you think of your current situation and life, and what gets you feeling like that in the first place? Is it spending time with certain people, doing certain kinds of work, eating in certain restaurants or going to certain gym classes, where it seems like everyone else looks like Barbie and Ken? What is making you feel worse about yourself?

Sometimes, receiving feedback or criticism from others is a trigger. When you feel hurt or upset by someone's feedback, know that's just their perception (just like how in the beginning of the book we went through what your perceptions may be). There may be times when someone gives you feedback or attempts to criticise you and it rolls off you like water off a duck's back; then at other times it sticks to you, clinging to your self-confidence and triggering deep-seated fears of your unworthiness.

When this happens, it's actually a beautiful chance for you to ask yourself what's being triggered in you. If you feel upset by something someone has said, it's often because it's tapped into a deeper fear or concern you hold about your personality or an aspect of yourself or your life that you don't feel comfortable with. Your first reaction may be anger, which is okay, you're putting up a barrier to protect yourself, lest someone see inside your fragile heart.

Perhaps it doesn't go like that for you. While this comes down to how you feel about yourself on an inner level (maybe it's less about external factors or others' feedback), it's still a good idea to reduce or avoid certain triggers if possible. At least work with whatever aspect of yourself you're feeling triggered by, so you can build your self-confidence and sense of worthiness up again.

Dream really, really, really big

Now that you know your triggers, have sent some love and compassion to yourself and others, and gotten offline a little and back into the real world, it's time to ramp up the self-respect and self-worth, and the action-taking god/goddess inside you. It's time to dream, dream and dream.

What do you really want in your life? Is it an updated website, deeper friendships and relationships, more time off, an overseas holiday or just a deeper sense of inner freedom and harmony?

Dreaming about and visualising what you want will bring you many steps closer to seeing this come to fruition in your own life. There's no point in comparing yourself to someone else, if you're not actually going to go out and create what you want for yourself. And the first step in that process is knowing what you want. So, what is it that you really, truly, deeply want? Focus on your own work and life, focus on yourself, focus on your energy, then go out and make stuff happen.

Map out your own path, and then take action

Now that you've dreamed big (and bigger!) it's time to map out your own path and take action. What can you do today, tomorrow, this week and this month, to start moving towards what you want? What do you need to let go of?

And yes, this may mean letting go of a dream you've been holding onto, but don't really feel aligned to anymore. This is big, beautiful stuff. Let it go. If it was a big dream you're letting go of, think how much more beauty can take its place.

Surround yourself with people who believe in you

Sometimes I just need to call up a friend and vent. Although it's my mission to help you find validation from within, having good people around you to lean on is incredibly validating and helpful. Who can you call up and say, 'Oh my gosh, I'm feeling so low and my comparison is out of control!'? You might not even need their advice, just an open ear, a kind heart and a warm shoulder to cry (or talk) on.

Don't resist it ... be directed by it

Okay, here's where I give you slightly contradictory advice. Comparison can actually be helpful in certain circumstances, if you know how to work with it. The best way to work with comparison in this way is to **use it or lose it**. While it may be hard to fathom right now, there will be times in your life, or situations with certain people in your life, where a little bit of 'friendly envy' can be beneficial.

It might spur you on to finish your cover letter and send your resume in for a job you don't think you'll get, as a friend who was feeling a similar way about a possible job sent in their resume and landed the job that week. It might encourage you to take steps you wouldn't have thought you'd take, but you're encouraged because of something a friend, colleague or family member has recently done.

If you can use comparison in a friendly, lighthearted way to benefit yourself, while simultaneously sending out positive vibes to your so-called 'competitors', go for it.

⚶ A rising tide lifts all the boats ⚶

There is an old adage that says: *A rising tide lifts all the boats.* With the mindset changes I've outlined in this chapter, you'll be able to see what's holding you back and keeping you in swirling patterns of comparison, envy and self-judgement.

When you accept that the people you're comparing yourself to are just people—exactly like me and you—you'll give yourself permission to rise with them, not against them.

If you can find your triggers, send love out to those who you envy, be compassionate with yourself, know you'll get there when the time is right and, most importantly, map out your own path, dream your own dreams and visualise your own golden future, then you're onto a winning formula.

Whatever you need to do to release your comparison, give yourself permission to do it. If it means taking action in some area of your life, take action. If it's inspiring you to do something you never thought you would do or could do, jump on it. If it means taking a back seat and funnelling your energy into your own life, do that. What do you need to do? When can you start?

Releasing Comparison
WORKSHEET

I am currently comparing myself to:

....

....

I think it's because:

....

....

I feel triggered by:

....

....

What I see in this person's work/life/personality etc. that I really want is:

....

....

I know that I can have this too. My biggest dream is:

....

....

To make this happen, my next step is:

....

....

Taking action will allow me to feel:

....

....

And then the very next thing I'll do to align myself to what I want is:

....

....

I will send myself love by doing/giving/telling/showing myself:

....

....

I will send this person love by:

....

....

And then I'll feel:

....

....

Chapter 7

it's worth it

In my life I've discovered that if I cling to the notion that something's not possible, I'm arguing in favor of limitation. And if I argue for my limitations, I get to keep them.

Gay Hendricks, *The Big Leap*

There's something that many of us find hard to grasp. It's this idea that our worth is innate, that we don't have to earn it. Instead, we mask our fears and insecurities behind perfectionism and procrastination, thinking that's the only way to stave off the inevitable; that the world will see through us and realise we're a fraud and a fake, not worthy of having what we have right now; and that it'll all be taken away from us because we didn't do enough to keep it.

But this idea isn't just an idea. It's the **truth**. The truth is you are worthy, and once you believe it, you'll be able to fly so much higher on the winds of your own life.

No matter where you are on your journey, I'm sure a part of you desires to feel truly worthy of being where you are, of being who you are, and of really receiving what you desire. And really, that's probably why something in you felt called to pick up this book; because you know you can feel something more deeply, connect with yourself in a kinder way and ultimately change your mindset, redirect your energy and align to your true purpose in this life.

So many of us forget this when we're pushing ourselves to the limit and constantly comparing ourselves to others. We don't believe that we're already so worthy, without having to actually lift a finger or win the award or get the job or win someone over.

When we don't feel worthy or confident in ourselves, we don't allow ourselves to reach our full potential. And I'm sure you don't want to feel so misaligned or blocked to your potential or purpose anymore.

The lower our self-worth, the more we block ourselves from love, abundance, generosity, inner wisdom and guidance, because we intrinsically feel we don't deserve it. From this viewpoint, we are sure to sabotage ourselves if we feel we're getting too close to happiness, success, love and good fortune.

We're placing an **upper limit** on ourselves, as Gay Hendricks says in *The Big Leap*. And there are many ways we place this limit on ourselves, many ways to deflect and lower our self-worth. We believe in our own limitations, and so we then keep ourselves stuck exactly where we are.

We put up barriers to receiving more support from others, because we think we don't deserve it. Sometimes we don't even try for the next rung on the ladder, because we think we'll either fall or fail to reach it. We tell ourselves stories about things that aren't true, that haven't happened yet, that will **never** happen. We worry ourselves into an early emotional grave; we shut down and shut off because waking up to our true selves can feel terrifying and uncertain, and uncertainty is a deep dark well that we don't want to even peer into.

Another way we do this, when we're not feeling confident, is by sabotaging our very best efforts. When I was in the throes of comparison, I would sabotage myself by spending so much energy looking at other peoples' work, I could no longer see my own work or vision. That's hardly useful for attaining success and happiness in life.

The value of valuing yourself

In *The Untethered Soul*, author Michael A. Singer put it beautifully when he said:

> *Do not doubt your ability to remove the root cause of the disturbances inside of you. It really can go away. You can look deep within yourself, to the core of your being, and decide that you don't want the weakest part of you running your life.*

When I decided to release myself from the trap I'd placed myself in, to really look at the weakest part of me, the part that was telling me I couldn't have something because someone else already had it, the part of me who was constantly thinking everyone around me was so much better than I was, I immediately started to really value myself. I started to value not just who I was, but what I believed in. And I realised that—incredibly—I already believed in myself.

On one hand, I believe you must **value yourself** before anything else is truly possible in your life. On the other hand, the only way I could start to really value myself, my gifts, my creativity, my intuition and my own path was by giving myself permission do just that: value myself above all else, before I thought I was ready, and give myself the chance to start a new path by letting go of comparison, the part of me that kept me weak, small and meek.

Undervaluing ourselves doesn't just mean we think lowly or poorly of ourselves. It also means we give others permission to treat us poorly or abuse our boundaries. We put people on pedestals but we keep ourselves way below where we'd like to be.

When I tidied up my boundaries and started to really value myself, a few amazing things happened (apart from finally ceasing the daily comparison!). I fostered amazing new friendships in my work sphere, which propelled me forward and felt so supportive; I rebranded one of my eCourses, updated the content and had an insanely successful launch, that saw me earning the same in one month that I'd earned in my first year of clinical practice; and my client calendar went from steady to abundantly overflowing and booked out weeks in advance, with a long waiting list. Not only that, but I'd just increased the prices of my 1:1 sessions by 50%, and I was still booked out.

This wasn't just a lovely coincidence. This was me valuing myself, owning my worth, making space for what I truly wanted, aligning myself to abundance and knowing deeply that there wasn't **just enough** for me, there was **more than enough** to go around. Just because someone else had something, that wasn't a reason I couldn't have it. It was simply shining a light on what I knew I could have too.

Why do so many of us suffer in silence with low self-worth, undervaluing our talents? I think much of it has to do with our constant worrying, perfectionism and tendency to continue pushing ourselves until we have nothing left to give, and then some. When we feel deeply unworthy, the next step is a lack of empowerment and a big shot of self-sabotage.

Even though we may be feeling undervalued and in turn undervaluing ourselves, we may still be trying to prove ourselves. And this constant desire to prove ourselves often affects us on many levels.

You may already know a little about how our emotions affect us physically, and vice versa. So I'd like to deepen that knowledge (or invite you into the amazing world of metaphysical anatomy) and give you an idea of how your lack of self-worth may be affecting you.

ᐰ Manifestations of over-proving ourselves ᐰ

Low self-worth may manifest in our bodies in many different ways. If we're looking at the physical signs, this may come up for you as adrenal fatigue, burnout and just a general malaise or low-grade constant fatigue, because you're constantly pushing yourself. I also see it come up as issues surrounding food and body image, e.g. binging, purging, starving, over-exercising and constantly worrying about your health and your body. It can also show up as digestive issues and gut imbalances, such as candida. In *Metaphysical Anatomy*, author Evette Rose likens candida to an energetic sponge; it's often drawn to and thrives on negative emotions and thoughts, including low self-worth and negative self-talk.

On a spiritual level, when we don't feel worthy we're blocking ourselves from listening to and following our true selves, our higher guidance, our inner guide and our wisdom. We do this often because we're so stuck in the muck of trying to guide ourselves out of wherever we are, we forget we can ask for help from something higher and greater and wisdom-filled, something like … the universe, our inner guide and wisdom. We must lean into being able to ask ourselves for advice and wisdom, and then really listen to it, to the part of us that knows we're worthy and just wants to say it aloud.

On a mental and emotional level, low self-worth can manifest as anxiety, depression, lack of focus and commitment, and a wishy-washy sense of not knowing your purpose or lacking the drive and motivation to follow your heart and dreams. Of course, there are many causes and contributing factors to depression, anxiety and mental health issues, so please don't think I'm saying only low self-worth is causing these. There's often a bi-directional pathway with emotional and physical issues, e.g. depression is a cause and a consequence of inflammation in the body, and inflammation is a cause and a consequence of depression. So in the same way, one could say low self-worth and a lack of confidence can exacerbate depression or show up more strongly because of it.

Either way, it's so important to seek help if you're feeling low and depressed. And know this: the world needs you. We need your spark and your love and your light. And you have this spark, this love, and this light already inside you. We may have to peel back some layers so it shines out, but it's already there in you.

Self-sabotage and secondary gains

How many times in your life have you wondered how things may have turned out if you were a better, more deserving person? If you don't get the job you really wanted, do you think it's because you're not good enough? If the relationship breaks down, do you think it's because you aren't deserving of love? If things don't go to plan, do you find yourself nodding in agreement with the ways things panned out, as you never thought you'd be able to have what you want anyway?

If so, I'd like to welcome you to the world of self-sabotage and secondary gains. You may be aware of these concepts or they might be completely new to you. To help you understand that you're worthy, you need to understand what could be blocking you from feeling worthy. So let's look at that now.

Self-doubt and a lack of self-confidence and low self-worth tie in strongly to self-sabotage. If you don't have confidence in yourself or if you don't believe that you can do something, you'll sabotage your very best chances of making it happen.

In the world of kinesiology, we call these concepts of self-sabotage and secondary gains 'blocks'. Think of them as blocks to you feeling the way you want to feel, aligning yourself with what you truly want, and attracting and manifesting positive things into your life.

Most of the time, sabotaging ourselves isn't a completely conscious choice—I mean, why would we **choose** to sabotage ourselves? But sometimes we do, and whether it's conscious or not, we understand this through the lenses of both self-sabotage and secondary gains. Once understood, you can start to release these from your life.

ᴄ‌ᴏ Understanding self-sabotage ᴄ‌ᴏ

Self-sabotage is a block to getting where we want to be in our lives. It's where you consciously or subconsciously don't think you deserve something, so you derail your best-laid plans or interrupt any chance of creating or attracting what you truly want.

For instance, you start a fight with your partner the moment you sit down to a romantic dinner; you reverse your car into a pole the day you get an unexpected bonus, and the cost of fixing your car is **exactly** the same amount as your bonus (this has happened to me—good times); you enter a competition but you keep telling friends, 'Oh, I won't win, I won't win!' and then you don't win and you tell them, 'Oh see, I knew it! I knew I wouldn't win!' You spill coffee on yourself as you're walking into the important job meeting or you miss your flight on the holiday of your dreams.

These are all instances where the outcome could have been completely different, completely in our favour ... yet for some reason, things turned out less than best. On some level, we've done this to ourselves; on another level, we can shift and clear this in order to release the self-sabotaging behaviour, so that next time we align ourselves to something we want, we have a real chance of getting it (or something better).

And how's this for Divine timing, in terms of spot-on stories to include in my book? Just this morning after my workout, I drove down to the beach to grab a coffee from my favourite cafe. I saw a car about to pull out of a car space, so I sat idly about ten metres away with my indicator light on, waiting to take its place. After several minutes of waiting, I felt something bash into my car. I got such a fright and quickly turned to my right to see a P-plate driver (a driver who's recently got their licence) with his bumper stuck into the passenger door of my car. This was clearly an excellent way to start my weekend.

We both hopped out of our cars, and I asked him for his licence and details, so we could sort it out. He said to me, 'Oh, this is a great way to start my birthday.' I apologised (even though he was the one who hit my car!) and wished him a happy birthday. He replied with, 'Doesn't matter, I knew something like this would happen; I was having way too nice a morning.' Huzza, self-sabotage in its finest form! I told him that at least this would never happen to him again, as he'd now reverse more slowly and look into his rear-view mirror (I know, annoying things adults say) and his response, again self-deprecating was, 'Knowing me, I **will** do this again.'

And with that perspective, you can be mighty sure he will.

Understanding secondary gains

Secondary gains are similar to self-sabotage in that they block us from having what we really want, but there's a little twist here. On some level, again either consciously or subconsciously, there is a hidden benefit to staying where you are.

For instance, perhaps each Monday when you get to work, you and your cute new colleague chat about your weekends. Perhaps you both discuss how much fun your weekend was, and have a little giggle about how hungover you feel, or how much unhealthy food you ate after being so good all week, or how you slept in for way too long. Maybe you really enjoy these conversations (doesn't hurt that your colleague is super cute and you're finally totally over your ex). However, if you were to suddenly create new patterns, and enjoy a healthier weekend and a more chilled-out lifestyle, which meant you ate and moved your body in a healthier, more consistent manner, you wouldn't be able to have these mutual chats on a Monday with your cute colleague. Then what else would you talk about? What would happen to your awesome connection?

What you're gaining by staying in this less-than-healthy pattern is a connection with another human that feels safe and secure. Your cycle of weekly clean eating and then weekend chocolate overindulgences (not that there's anything wrong with a chocolate treat!) keeps you connected to someone you care about. Clearing this cycle might feel scary, so it's easiest (and beneficial) for you to stay exactly where you are.

Self-sabotage and secondary gains have played a role in my life too

The reason you're reading this book is because I overcame a self-sabotaging thought pattern. A little while ago, I attended the *Hay House Writer's Workshop*. After the workshop, we had three months to write and submit our proposal. Yet for most of those three months, I nearly talked myself out of writing it.

For some reason, even though I had a good feeling about this book deal deep down in my heart, I kept telling myself things like: *If I submit my proposal, I won't be able to launch my Heartfelt Harmony® Society courses and guides, because people won't want to read my book and enrol in my courses. If I submit my proposal, I won't know how to keep planning the rest of my year, until I know the outcome.*

Ah, the stuff we tell ourselves!

Yet all through this negative (and incredibly unhelpful) self-talk, I still had this persistent thought that I should enter the competition.

One day, just over a week before the submission date, my inner critic faded into the background and my inner ally popped her head up and said, *Um, Cass? You keep saying you have a good feeling about this book deal but you haven't written the proposal yet. So … hop to it!*

The universe rearranged my calendar so I had all this unexpected space, I wrote my proposal that week, and it's turned into this book you're reading.

In my case, I had both self-sabotage and secondary gains at play. The self-sabotage was the negative self-talk that told me I didn't know how to write a book (stemming from a lack of confidence, merely because I hadn't written a book before). The secondary gains came in to play when I incorrectly told myself that my book would mean people wouldn't want to enrol in my online *Heartfelt Harmony® Society* courses and guides.

The perceived hidden benefit to not writing the book was that my online courses would be able to do well. Yet in truth, that made no logical sense. It was like me saying that if you walked into a grocery store and grabbed a bag of apples, you wouldn't want to buy any pears too, because you already had apples. This notion was merely a construct of my own fearful ego, determined to keep me well and truly stuck where I was.

Gratefully, the higher, wiser part of me realised this is in due course, and with enough time to write my proposal. So here we are, thankfully!

Let's help you listen to the higher, wiser part of yourself and feel incredibly worthy too, okay?

✧ Sparks of awareness ✧

One of the best ways to clear out old, negative self-sabotaging behaviour or secondary gains that may be blocking your self-worth and empowerment is to bring awareness to what's going on under the surface. One way to do this is through energetic healing such as kinesiology, as well as taking the time to get to know yourself and giving yourself space to gain greater insight into your own behaviour through meditation and journaling. You can use the questions coming up in a juicy journaling session, or read through them and then sit in silent contemplation, making space to allow for fresh new insights to surface.

One thing I don't suggest doing is ignoring these questions, even if they feel annoying and grate against you, even if resistance pops its head up. If you're undervaluing yourself and sabotaging yourself, the greatest thing you can do for your ego (who's happily and smugly keeping you rooted in fear, resistance and resentment) is block any new insights coming to light by ignoring or brushing over these questions.

I suggest sitting down to think about the questions when you have a little time afterwards to sit in stillness and let the insights integrate, shift and sift through your body. This will help you start clearing these stresses and blocks now, so that you can have a more positive experience and outcome from reading this book.

Yes, it may take around half an hour to write your answers out, but imagine all the stuff that'll stay stuck in you if you don't work through them. Self-sabotage, anyone?

Here are some questions to help in clearing sabotage and secondary gains:

- What's currently going on for me right now that's affecting my worth, or that I think is happening because I don't feel worthy?
- How would I prefer this situation to pan out?
- How am I getting in my own way with this?
- How would I benefit if I felt more worthy?
- Who else would benefit if I felt more worthy (or insert whatever else you want to feel)?
- If I really did feel more worthy and valued, and I changed an aspect of my life, what would I miss out on? (If you can answer this question, you're shining a light on a benefit in staying exactly where you are.)
- Is there a benefit in staying where I am? What could this be? Is it real, or just fear playing out?

- What's the best thing that could happen to me if I felt more worthy? How would this affect my life?
- What's the worst thing that could happen to me if I felt more worthy? How would this affect my life?
- How can I let go of this fear or worry, and find the benefit in feeling more worthy instead?
- What would happen if I let go of ... e.g. feeling unworthy or invaluable (or insert your own word here)?
- What can I change or let go of in my life, in order to feel more worthy?
- Who would feel threatened or upset if I felt more worthy and confident?
- What would I be able to do if I felt more worthy, that I feel I can't do right now?
- What would life look like if I felt incredibly worthy and self-confident and acted from this space and energy?
- What can I do right now to allow myself to feel more worthy? Do I need to move my body? Have a conversation with someone? Take action somewhere in my life? Create some extra space in my life?

Integrating new insights and awareness

Now spend a little time in stillness and quiet, or with some calming, relaxing music on, to allow for new insights to drop in, to reflect, and to integrate your new awareness.

Perhaps new insights and awareness will drop in instantly, or perhaps they'll slowly trickle in over a couple of days, or both. We're all different and these 'blocks' will clear for us at different stages in our journey. You might feel energetic shifts or emotional blocks release the moment you read something, or see something, or breathe in a beautiful essential oil blend. It might be journaling, massage, yoga or a good, deep chat with a girlfriend that clears stuff or shifts certain blocks for you.

If answering these questions felt difficult, tiresome or stirred up some raw emotions, that's okay. Let it stir, rumble and shift stuff inside you. Let what needs to seep, be absorbed with love. Let what needs to shift, be transmuted and transformed and released, gracefully and gratefully. Let what needs to be sowed, be planted and reaped at the best possible time, for your highest, most precious good.

Sometimes the only way up to the light is through the darkness, and darkness is only scary when we don't know what it's hiding. Through answering these questions, you'll shine a light on what's keeping you stuck, you'll see you're not hiding anything that difficult, or scary, or insurmountable. You'll see how capable, insightful, brilliant and bold you are. You'll feel validated, deeply and truly and innately. And while sometimes the only way to see this is with hindsight, hindsight is better than no sight at all.

Chapter 8

worth without accomplishments

❦

If we start to understand that we don't need to earn our worth or do anything to prove how valuable we are, then on the flip side, we must also understand that nothing can remove our worth and value, not even ourselves.

❧ You're already worthy ☙

A funny thing happens when we start to believe that we're already worthy; signs of worth, abundance and joy flow into our life every single day. They may have always been there, but now we start to notice them more frequently. We have more 'good' days than 'bad', good things start flowing to us, from the simple (a car spot right outside your favourite cafe) to the mighty (your business starts thriving even though you haven't changed a thing ... except your mindset).

It's time to transform your mindset and step fully into your own self-worth, so that you can start to enjoy the flow of life that only you can create for yourself. It's time to start believing in yourself, backing yourself and accepting yourself, telling yourself you're worthy and then truly believing it. This will help you release comparison so much more easily, because you'll actually believe that you can have what you desire too, and that there's space for you.

ᖇᖇ You can't earn it, so you can't lose it ᖇᖇ

A little while ago, while on a month-long holiday through the USA, my husband and I went to watch his brother graduate from Harvard. One of the main speakers mentioned self-worth several times in her speech. One of her phrases really resonated with me: *You can't earn it with accomplishments, hence you can't lose it with failure.*

I love this idea so much. We can't earn our worth, so we can't lose our worth. We may misplace it, we may bury it under fear and worries, but with a little digging, we can find it again. With a little inner work, we'll see it's always been there, and it always will be.

The idea that we need to earn our worth both motivates and sustains us; yet it can also tear us down when we falsely think that we can lose it as punishment, if we believe we haven't done enough.

It's time to uplift your thoughts, and own your worth. Let's go through some things you can start doing in order to make space for yourself in your own world.

◁ Release your perfectionism ▷

When I was in kindergarten, about five years old, my teacher told my parents I'd be my own worst enemy because I was such a perfectionist. I'd colour outside the lines and freak out. Since then, I've made a certain peace with this aspect of myself and I now never allow it to stop me from doing something because I think it's not perfect enough. I'm more than happy to release things into the world, and I trust I've always done my best with what I had … but I still like colouring inside the lines.

We'll talk about perfectionism again soon, but it would be remiss of me to not include it here, because our perfectionism tendencies are so tied up with our self-worth and sense of personal value. I know this because so many of my clients tell me they feel unworthy because of their perfectionist tendencies and, of course, I've felt it too.

My clients tell me they constantly worry they're not doing enough to earn their own worth, and as such, they push their sense of self-worth down so low, hiding it in the deepest corner of themselves because they don't trust it enough to shine a light on it. When I speak to them of worthiness and empowering themselves in our sessions, they tell me of their worries and fears that they'll never live up to their own incredibly high expectations.

If we feel low, we think one way to get out of our lull is to set new, better, higher goals—goals that we may or may not reach, and goals that might feel so out of reach for where we are in life (not impossible, just not really plausible … yet). Then if we don't reach these goals, we blame and shame ourselves. We tell ourselves we're even less worthy than we initially imagined and now we've really gone and blown it and ruined things for ourselves.

When we create higher expectations of ourselves from this state of a lack of empowerment, from the ledge of a perfectionist's view, we often act in ways that further promote this lack of empowerment. We're cruel to ourselves, we put ourselves down. We block our chances of allowing ourselves to feel valued, validated, recognised and worthy.

By telling ourselves we're not good enough, we hold ourselves back from having self-confidence, a deep connection to ourselves, and clarity about what we desire.

Accept compliments and love from others

Deflecting compliments and praise from others is another way we block ourselves from feeling worthy. Your mission, should you choose to accept it, is to acknowledge this, so that next time someone says something lovely about you, you reply 'Thank you', even if that feels like the hardest thing in the world. On an important level, when you do this you're raising your vibration and your self-worth. I know it's sometimes easier said than done, however it's so very possible and important for you, so set your mind to it and open your heart to it.

Know yourself and acknowledge what makes you happy

You can start to validate yourself and increase your sense of worth by discovering what makes you happy, and honouring this side of yourself. This is one of my top recommendations to clients when they're feeling a little low; I ask them to take some time out from their busy lives and schedules and just indulge in whatever feels amazing to them, **guilt free**. That's the kicker. It doesn't mean you need to quit your job and book a one-way ticket to Thailand, but it does mean you need to devote yourself to your own self-care and self-worth, by looking after yourself in a way that feels right to you.

For me, this meant acknowledging parts of myself that I'd tried to hide or squash down, throughout my teens and early twenties. You see, I used to feel so guilty for not going out to nightclubs, but I hated clubbing. I felt so separate and disconnected from my friends, but I had so many other ideas of what was fun, and clubbing was not one of them. Choosing to go home early on a Saturday night before my friends went out to bars and clubs made me feel unworthy, even though I was also filled with relief at being able to go home, but only until I realised it's okay to not like it. Once I replaced that with doing things that felt wonderful, and honoured myself without feeling guilty for it, my self-worth skyrocketed.

Is there something in your life that you love doing or that makes you feel really happy, but you give yourself a hard time about it? What can you do to incorporate this into your life in a way that feels pleasurable to you, and affirms your worth?

Uplift your thoughts to own your worth

So many of us feel we have to be perfect before we can deem ourselves worthy. Yet in reality, when we truly feel into our worth, we see we are already imperfectly perfect as we are.

I know this can sound impossible when there's so much going on for you in your life, when your mind feels like a whirlwind of stress, worry and trapped emotions, trying to find your sense of confidence and inner-belief can feel so foreign. If you're someone who constantly doubts yourself, you don't need to give yourself a hard time about it. Instead, start to see your doubts as little flags that point out where you can start to empower yourself and embody your greatest potential and the highest version of yourself.

When you start to do this, and live with self-confidence, you'll be able to make decisions from a place of deep inner knowing and confidence, and you'll find you question yourself, second-guess and doubt yourself less.

ᴇᴍ Empower yourself ᴄᴍ

Feeling empowered comes from within. Remind yourself each and every day that you are worthy. Remind the people around you, the people you spend time with each day, and the people you love and admire. Remind yourself in the good times, during times of struggle and during times of great success and happiness, knowing that you're capable of higher and higher levels of happiness, success, love, abundance and more.

To help you remind yourself daily, here are some affirmations you may like to work with:

- ᴍ *I am worthy*
- ᴍ *I'm 100% aligned to feeling worthy*
- ᴍ *I'm 100% aligned to knowing I'm worthy*
- ᴍ *My worth is innate*
- ᴍ *I am enough*
- ᴍ *I am doing enough*
- ᴍ *I'm in the right place*
- ᴍ *I'm on the right path*
- ᴍ *I'm doing my best*

To help you really align your energy to these affirmations, I'd like you to do a little journaling activity to clear any energetic stress around them. You know how sometimes you choose an affirmation, but even as you say it over and over again you can feel your body and energy stressing or tensing?

I'd like to help you clear those stresses first, so working with your chosen affirmation is even more helpful.

In a kinesiology session we set what we call goals, which are kind of like positive affirmations. Then we align your energy to these goals to create more flow and ease in your life, to allow you to get closer to where you want to be. The affirmations I've given you here are very similar to the kinds of goals we set in a kinesiology session.

So choose some of these affirmations (whichever ones resonate with you the most), write them down in a journal or notebook, and then answer the following questions to clear any stress that may surround these goals/affirmations:

1. Do I believe this affirmation can be true for me?
2. If not, why? What's blocking me from believing this?
3. What needs to change so I can start to believe and accept this?
4. Is there anything I can do right now that will help me feel into this goal, e.g. do I need to move my body a certain way, meditate, journal, speak to someone, let go of something?
5. What would change in my life if I believed this goal? Am I fearful of that, or do I welcome this change?
6. What's the best outcome of this affirmation or goal?

You can use these affirmations in any way that feels right for you. Say them daily, pin them up on your bathroom mirror or fridge, write them on a post-it and stick it on your computer, or even set a reminder on your phone for a certain time each day with one of the affirmations, so it pops up and you have to look at it. In this way, you're reminding yourself of your worth every day.

Transcend your blocks

Rise above them and seek a higher perspective. Everything you're going through is perfect and necessary for you to grow, heal, thrive and become the very best version of yourself. So sometimes the best thing to do is to make a commitment to transcend, to see what's blocking you and rise above it, to set new intentions, and create new paths forward. You can do this; you're worthy of knowing how worthy you are and acting from this space.

When you feel empowered, you can do anything

When you own your worth, when you can start to notice and release self-sabotages and secondary gains, and when you can truly feel into the empowered sense of self that is your birthright—that is, you don't need to do anything new or shiny or fancy to earn your own worth—then you'll be able to take great leaps in your life.

Here is a short meditation you can start to use to change your mindset, clear blocks and step fully into your worth. You can use this meditation at any time, and in any way that feels good to you. The focus of this meditation is the solar plexus chakra, which is our energy centre relating to self-worth, self-confidence, self-acceptance, personal power and empowerment. We'll talk about chakras a little later on.

Whichever way you work with this, I suggest keeping a notebook or journal nearby. Spend a few minutes at the end of the meditation to either jot down any insights that came up for you during the meditation, or to simply sit in a quiet meditation to reflect and allow for some integration time.

Here are four suggested ways to work with this meditation (always do what feels right to you):

1. Start your day by reading through this meditation a couple of times, then sit in stillness integrating its energy and messages for a couple of minutes (or as long as feels good to you). Then open your journal and free write, to release cleared, stored blocks and start listening to your guidance (who totally knows you're worthy).

2. Read over this before going to sleep, then sit in stillness for a couple of minutes before falling asleep, to allow the changes to integrate through the night.

3. Record yourself saying this meditation on your phone and listen to it at any time.

4. Download a free recording of this meditation from my website, at www.elevatevitality.com.au/you-are-enough-audio

~ You are Enough Meditation ~

The purpose of this meditation is to help you begin to trust yourself, and know that you are enough, as you are right now. In your busy mind and busy world, it's possible you've forgotten this, or let yourself believe that you need to do more in order to be more. So take this time now to sit in stillness, to sit and breathe, to sit and recalibrate. Begin by remembering something that has always, always been true, something that will always be true ... that you are enough.

To begin this meditation, sit in a comfortable position, either on a cushion, yoga mat, or with your back against a wall or chair so that you're very comfortable. Place your hands either in your lap, or on your knees, palms facing up, so you're able to receive what you need.

Take a few deep breaths in through your nose, and out through your mouth. Begin to feel your body settle and calm into this healing space, and as you do, start taking slightly deeper, longer, slower breaths in through your nose, and out through your nose.

Begin to visualise yourself becoming enveloped in a bright, warm, golden, yellow light. As it envelops you, you trust that this light is safe for you. It feels deeply comforting, healing and cleansing. It begins to flow through your body from the crown of your head, down through your forehead, brow and face, relaxing every muscle as it moves through your body. It continues to flow down through your throat area, your shoulders, your chest and heart, to your stomach, around to your back, down through your hips, your legs, knees, ankles and feet.

It flows in and through you with each deep breath in through your nose. As it washes through your body, it picks up anything that's feeling heavy, stuck or stagnant, any stress, overwhelm, tension, tightness and perfectionism. It also shines a light on what is causing or creating this heaviness. What is making you feel that you are not enough? Offer it up to this golden light to pick up, absorb or wash away.

This golden light starts to balance, align and clear your entire energy system, allowing you to feel more worthy, more confident, more trusting of yourself ... allowing yourself to believe that you are enough.

It continues to slowly fill every cell in your body. As it does, it infuses in you a deep sense of contentment, happiness, self-confidence and self-assurance.

Visualise it flowing through you, watch as it penetrates the deepest, darkest corners of your being, wherever you feel there is some darkness, heaviness or stuckness. Where do you need direct this light? Where can you breathe in this golden, yellow lightness?

It shines a light on any self-sabotaging behaviour or on any areas of your life where it feels safer to stay where you are, even though on some level you know that taking a leap forwards is where you want to go.

As you continue to breathe in this yellow light with each inhalation, allow your exhalations to clear and cleanse all you no longer need. Your worries, concerns and fears start to come to the surface, in order to be released and let go with every exhalation.

Now say to yourself: 'I am enough. I've done enough. I am powerful, confident and worthy.'

What can you do to align yourself to these powerful intentions?

As you feel your mind, body and spirit start to align to these intentions, you feel waves of clarity wash through you. Your mind feels light, bright and clear. The golden light empowers and lifts you up out your situation, so you can see a higher perspective.

You feel something shifting in your energy, as you realise what you can let go of now. And letting this go feels safe. It allows you to feel stronger, more worthy and more on soul purpose. You're able to start seeing how your vision for your future is manifesting; blocks you felt so intensely just moments before start to disappear from view.

Take several more deep breaths in and out, absorbing the beautiful yellow rays. What insights are coming to you now? Spend a few moments in silence now, allowing these insights and shifts in perception to come to the surface. Know that you are so worthy.

Trust that you are 100% aligned to stepping into your sense of worthiness, to feeling empowered and to acting in your highest integrity.

Feel yourself coming back into your body, back into this space and time, feeling worthy, feeling confident, feeling excited and grateful to be you … and open your eyes when you're ready.

In the next chapter we'll look at how you can stop the striving and start loving and accepting yourself right now, as well as ways to help you release the mindset that striving for your self-worth is non-negotiable, and help you create softer, more loving mindsets and attitudes to take forward into your life of empowerment and worthiness.

Part Two

releasing old attitudes +
adopting new mindsets

Chapter 9

you can stop the striving

༺༻

By now I'm sure you're coming to the realisation that perfectionism, low self-worth and feeling that you need to be doing more in order to be more are major themes in this book. So now it's time to move into how you can start releasing these old patterns and attitudes and adopt new mindsets, so you can transform the way you do your work in this world, the way you love yourself and others, and the way you show up every day.

Hopefully by now, there's a part of you that's softening to the idea that you don't need to push yourself as hard as you currently are, always giving yourself a hard time about even your very best efforts.

When you set out to achieve a goal, do you have a preconceived idea of how it should pan out? Do you like things to go a certain way? Do you find yourself becoming attached to dreams, desires, outcomes or goals? How do you feel if things don't pan out the way you wanted them to? Does not knowing what the future holds make you want to control every moment of it?

If you answered 'yes' to any of those questions, welcome to the world of striving, perfectionism, control and attachment. In the past, I'd have invited you into my council and we could have run this world together. But jokes aside, I totally know how it feels to control, grip tighter and try to drive your dreams in certain ways, and then feel flattened when things don't turn out the way you expected, the way you hoped, and the way you dreamed they would.

In the past I've sometimes pushed myself a little too much. At times I realised this, and at other times I just stayed on autopilot; I didn't realise I was being so hard on myself, so how could I soften?

Whether I was striving for my own affection and accolades or someone else's, the result was the same: set a goal, race towards it, feel crushed if I didn't meet it, abuse and berate and punish myself for not being good enough. This goal could have been based on my work, my weight or my worth; it was all the same.

I know there's a better way now. I know that just as we can acknowledge ourselves each and every day, so too we can acknowledge our growth and achievements as we progress, instead of waiting for the finishing line that we never even let ourselves cross.

Because I know what this can be like, pushing ourselves to breaking point, and giving ourselves such a hard time about it, I now know what to look out for. I want to help you release these old patterns and mindsets too. I also know that pushing ourselves doesn't make us feel more worthy ... it makes us feel **less** worthy. And it never ends, until we decide we don't want to let it run our lives.

As we discussed in the previous chapter, we can't earn our worth so we can't lose it. Yet there have been so many times in my life where I feel like I've gambled my self-worth against a false perception that I'll be better if I keep pushing. And when I've lost the gamble, I've been left hurt, confused and wounded.

I know that pushing myself doesn't leave me feeling light or full of clarity, and I know that pushing myself doesn't really allow me to move forwards in life in a simple, calm and enjoyable way. In fact, it's quite the opposite; striving causes joy to be reeled back in, confidence to be sucked dry and exhaustion to hit an all-time high.

Does striving for perfection make you perfect?

Brené Brown, author of *The Gifts of Imperfection*, says that perfectionism isn't the same as striving to be your best, or trying to improve yourself. She says it's destructive, because there is simply no such thing as perfect:

> *Perfectionism is a self-destructive and addictive belief system that fuels this primary thought: If I look perfect, live perfectly and do everything perfectly, I can avoid*

or minimize the painful feelings of shame, judgment and blame.

How many times in your life have you actually felt better or uplifted after pushing yourself? If you really think about it, most likely it left you feeling emptier and just pushed you to push yourself even more the next time. If you can't acknowledge how far you've come, how will you ever see ahead and visualise your future?

Sometimes we get confused; we think our constant striving for perfection is making us more perfect, or helping us reach higher and take bigger strides in our life. But I don't believe it does. Your level of perfectionism is not positively correlated to higher levels of acceptance and confidence. In fact, likely it's making you feel less confident and less worthy.

It's this striving for perfectionism that makes us feel like we're as far from perfect as possible. And the 'beauty and the beast' of it is that it all comes from somewhere inside us—that part of ourselves that thinks the only way to be better in our lives is to be hard on ourselves is on overdrive; the part that tells us not to rest when we're tired, or take a break when we feel mentally depleted and emotionally fragile. This is the side of us that pushes through physical exhaustion until we're injured, or gives us such a hard time that we lose all perspective and become resentful, bitter and teary. The part of ourselves that wants us to slow down, to rest, to be kinder and more compassionate gets drowned out by guilt, sorrow and shame.

It's not how I want to live, and it's not how I want you to live either. I want to you to know that you don't need to strive anymore; you are good enough as you are. When you pull back a little, when you ease up, when you go with the flow (I know—what is this thing called 'flow'?), things can actually turn out way better than you first imagined.

Questions to ask yourself:

- What am I striving for in my life?
- How is this affecting my life?
- What would happen if I were happy being imperfectly perfect, happy being me?
- How can I be a little gentler with myself? What will I tell myself the next time my perfectionist tries to control me?

Is your perfectionism driving you to exhaustion?

Do you ever find yourself thinking (perhaps just under the surface) that your constant striving is exhausting you? I did, in fact I remember very clearly one time where I was so blinded by this side of me that I was getting heart palpitations because I was so stressed.

There were many contributing factors to this. I was in the first couple of years of my business; I was studying for both a post-grad Human Nutrition degree at university as well as kinesiology; I was seeing clients, running online webinars, creating a brand-new online course and speaking at my first few corporate events. Had I taken on more than I could chew? Of course, but I was trying to chew it all at the same time, and almost choking on being overcommitted.

My desire for things to be perfect meant I put in extra time and hours where I either didn't need to, or wasn't expected to. As an example, I was hired to speak at a big event, and the organisers put me in charge of the menu and catering, so that I could have control over the food, ensuring that it was healthy and fit in with my suggestions.

Initially, this really excited me. But it soon became clear that I had taken on way more than I could handle. I'm not an events coordinator (and I now know I don't enjoy being one). This level of commitment added so much stress and pressure to my plate, and I wasn't being paid for all the extra time I put in meeting with caterers, creating menus, going back and forth and everything in between, which left me feeling quite resentful by the end of it and added to my stress.

By the time the event approached, my heart palpitations were worrying me no end. In fact, I even made an appointment with a cardiologist and had a 24-hour Holter monitor put in place, to check my heart was fine. Thankfully all was okay, and I was reminded of the myriad ways stress and striving affects us on so many levels.

I remember going home in the taxi right after the event and feeling so relieved, and it wasn't just because I'd finished the event, thoroughly enjoyed it and received wonderful feedback. It was because I knew I'd never take on something like that again; I had let my boundaries be overstretched and exhausted myself in the process.

How is your perfectionism or striving affecting you? Is your body craving rest, compassion and kindness? In reality, those are things we could all do with more of.

In a later chapter we'll look at burnout, boundaries and fatigue on a deeper level. But it's a good idea to start bringing awareness to how your striving is affecting you on a physical, mental, emotional and spiritual level now.

Chapter 10

always moving the goalposts

ᯤ

One thing about striving is that it can be endless if we let it. If you're someone who constantly 'moves the goalposts' so to speak, then we can be part of another club! It's called the *Always Moving the Goalposts Club*. We meet every single day, at any time, and we **never leave**!

To be a part of this club you must:

- ꙮ Be very hard on yourself
- ꙮ Never think you've done enough
- ꙮ Always keep pushing yourself (even through things like exhaustion, brain fog, overwhelm, injury, sickness, even on weekends and holidays, and even after you've accomplished your first and second and third goal)
- ꙮ Quite often move the goalposts, before you've even kicked your goals

⚘ Berate yourself for not reaching your goals (even though, let's be honest now, you'll never let yourself reach them if you always move them, right?)

Are you part of this club? If you are, I actually think we should stop meeting up. I'm really sorry about that, because I know you want the best for yourself, but I also know that what we put ourselves through as members of this club is not enjoyable, pleasurable, sustainable or beneficial in any way. (And it's actually not turning us into better versions of ourselves.)

I'm not saying we shouldn't have goals. I'm not saying we shouldn't celebrate our successes, or even create new goals as we accomplish previous ones. What I am saying is that we shouldn't keep running ourselves into the ground by never actually stopping and acknowledging what we've done, and how far we've come. It's time we allowed ourselves to be proud of what we've done, to honour ourselves and give ourselves a little break, a rest, a reward.

When you finally give yourself permission to stop moving your goalposts, you finally give yourself permission to stop striving.

One way to do this that I've found so successful with my own goals, and that my clients love as well, is to set **intentions** instead of hard goals, and dish them up with a big side serve of compassion, patience and trust.

Danielle LaPorte had an amazing idea when she set out her *Desire Map*. She says we shouldn't set goals, but rather work out how we want to feel, and work towards feeling that way.

By doing something like this, and by setting intentions and manifesting your true desires (or something better), you'll open yourself up to all the beautiful things that are coming your way that you may have missed in your attempt to rush ahead, unacknowledged and ungrounded.

Let's get familiar with intention setting now, and discover how to make it an enjoyable part of your life, because it truly is.

Chapter 11

intention setting 101

~~~

*No matter what is happening in our lives, we choose how
we wish to think about it. And the greatest gift we give
ourselves is often our willingness to change our minds ...
we have the power to believe that something else is possible,
that things can change, that a miracle can happen.*

Marianne Williamson, *The Law of Divine Compensation*

Guess what's so much nicer than striving and fighting and making things difficult for ourselves? Intention setting. Manifesting. Making space for what we want. Guess what happens when we do this? Wonderful, amazing, light-filled things happen to us and for us. We can flow, we can let go, and we can love where we're at. We feel full of trust and wisdom and intuition. We know we're on the right path and we trust that what comes to us is meant to, and that what we don't have yet, we just don't have ... yet. And it's for our highest good.

Intention setting may be new to you, or old news. Either way, it's a beautiful part of a beautiful life. So in this chapter, I'll share with you a few ways you can embrace intention setting to live a life full of worth, confidence, trust and faith.

When you set intentions, set intentions, then let them go

Your intentions will manifest and find their way back to you. Think of this like posting a letter, the old fashioned way. You don't really see how it gets from A to B, but you let the letter go and trust it'll find its way to where it needs to go.

Perhaps something even better will find its way to you. Perhaps the outcome won't look like the thing you thought you wanted, but it will be for the betterment of your soul. Perhaps it won't be on your time, but on Divine time. And can I let you in on a secret? Divine time is always **on time**.

Use the moon to manifest, and to let go

I love working with the cycles of the moon when I set intentions. Traditionally, the full moon is a great time to release what's no longer serving you, and the full moon is a time to set new intentions and plant seeds for what you want to sow later.

Here's how I work with the moon cycles:

New moon

I'll do a new moon meditation where I set intentions about what I wish to manifest. I'll make time to do some journaling, where I'll write out some of the intentions or goals that I wish to align myself to. I try not to make them outcome-based, e.g. instead of *I hope fifty people sign up to my eCourse,* I write something like, *I'm 100% aligned to the best and highest number of people signing up to my eCourse.*

I'll often place any crystals I'm working with outside overnight, under the light of the moon, to 'charge' their energy. Right before I do this, I'll cleanse them under purified water or with a sage stick so they carry no old energy, and are ready for my intentions to be placed in them (energetically). I'll teach you a little more about how to use crystals to support you later on in the book.

Full moon

At the full moon I'll do a full moon meditation, and then cleanse and charge my crystals and leave them out overnight, to help them release old energy.

I'll also either write down some things I wish to let go of, or set the intention that whatever I no longer need is safe to leave (this could be a mindset, a problem I'm experiencing or just a situation that could do with less focus and attention). I may also have some kind of energetic healing at this time. Perhaps a kinesiology session (either with my own kinesiologist and friend, Kerry Rowett from *Awaken Kinesiology*, or one I do on myself); a reiki healing or distant reiki healing (my go-to lady is my friend and healer, Sara Brooke from *The Space In Between*); or just have a long Epsom salts bath, a longer daily meditation session, a journaling session, go for a massage or a long walk in nature.

In this way I make space for whatever I no longer need to shift, release and be let go, in a really pleasurable way. Try it for yourself and see how you feel and how it works for you.

ℰ Make space for your desires to manifest ℘

I remember a client who came to me really worried about money. She was worried she wasn't saving enough, and felt as though she never had enough money.

One of my first questions I asked her was, 'Do you have a savings account?' She looked a little stunned, and then smiled, realisation spreading across her face. 'No, I don't,' she replied.

Straightaway we came to the same understanding; without intentional space for what she wanted, how would she ever receive it? She went out and opened a savings account that week, and the next time I saw her she felt so much more confident about her money and her ability to save.

There's an old saying: *Nature abhors a vacuum.* If you create space, something will fill it. On the flip side, if you have no space, where can you put anything? How can you manifest what you desire, if you don't have space for it in your life? What do you need to make space for?

As I glance up from my computer screen, I see a quote I've written on a pink post-it and stuck above my computer. It's from Danielle LaPorte, author of *The Desire Map* and *The Fire Starter Sessions*. The quote simply says: *Make room for the love that's sure to come.*

I see it every single day, and so every single day I'm reminded to make space, to clear, to cleanse, to align to what I want. Perhaps it's time you do something like this too.

Release your expectations

Just last night I bumped into a good friend of mine at a launch party. Our conversation turned to the topic of expectations. We're in the same industry and we both coach women from around the world through various stages of them finding themselves and owning their worth. And at the same time, we were giggling about how much running your own business is a test in releasing expectations.

It's one of the cornerstones of good intention setting: to set pure intentions, to put your heart into them, to align to them and then to **let them go**.

When I submitted my proposal for this book, I instantly let go of all expectations. I just submitted it, then let it go. I really believe I manifested this book, but the best thing is that I didn't attach to the goal or outcome on any level. I didn't obsess over it, or plan the rest of my year around whether I got the book deal or not. I didn't think about it every single day and I didn't tell myself everything would be ruined if I didn't get it.

I just set the intention, put it out there, aligned myself with positive, trusting thoughts, let it go, and allowed it come back to me in whichever form was right for me.

I know this sounds so much easier than it is, but having expectations of how you think things should pan out can be a huge, complicated and pricey recipe for disappointment. A much nicer way to think about things is to say this to yourself, to your intentions, to the universe: *I'm aligning myself to ... (insert intention here), or something better.*

Saying 'or something better' means that whatever transpires is for the betterment of yourself, your soul, your life. Saying 'or something better' means that you won't be disappointed; you'll be content. Saying 'or something better' means that you understand things don't always turn out the way we imagine or the way we think they should. They turn out how they need to, even if we can't see the blessings in them for the moment.

It can be easier, if you let it

You don't need to keep striving and struggling to prove yourself, and you don't need to attach yourself to your goals to feel worthy. When you believe you're enough, you give yourself permission to be enough, exactly as you are. This doesn't mean you stop learning, growing, or moving forwards or hitting new goals. It means your goals stop defining you. It means you reward yourself just for being you. It means you love yourself just because of who you are. It means you acknowledge you're simultaneously perfect and imperfect, and you know deeply that's the perfect way for you to be.

By setting intentions, releasing expectations and finding your own way of going with the flow, you'll be able to continue to align yourself to growth, advancement and progression without the self-scrutiny, perfectionism and internal struggle or hardships.

You can still be ambitious and successful. You can still create goals, set intentions and work towards them. You can still be the very best version of yourself. But you can choose to do this from a space of worth, empowerment and intuition, instead of pushing, striving and struggling.

This is made easier when you truly accept yourself and are able to be compassionate to yourself, which we're about to go through. This next chapter may call on you to examine how you really talk to yourself, and what you really think of yourself. Go make some tea, and let's dive in.

Chapter 12

struggle vs. surrender …
which one wins?

⁕

*When you stop struggling to make something go the way
you've wanted it to, you shift the energy grid of your
life. Facing the facts is liberating (even though it can be
wrenching)—and with that truth comes a major power surge.*

Danielle LaPorte

Sometimes we go through challenging times and we're
forced to take a really good look at how we're managing
our time, our energy and where our thoughts are taking
us. Sometimes struggling seems easier because we feel like
we're being productive, 'taking the bull by the horns' and
trying to make things better for ourselves, by trying to control
the situation, an outcome or even someone else.

We can't control many things in this world, but we can
look after our own thoughts. I don't even want to say we

can 'control' our thoughts, as I don't want to place a negative connotation on that concept.

It's interesting though, because when we're stuck in the cycle of struggle we can't see it clearly, or we think it's natural and normal to be thinking a certain way. How can we uplift our thoughts, if we don't even think they need to be uplifted? That's what happens when we're struggling sometimes. And by struggling I mean trying to control outcomes; being rigid in our thoughts and perspectives; holding on to past situations and events that we think haven't worked out in our favour (even though if we changed our perspective, we'd see it's possible they did) and worrying about them constantly; or trying to change the past by fighting with the present. I also often see my clients struggling when they're being uncompassionate and unforgiving with themselves.

Even if someone close to us points it out, we're quick to say things like: 'But you don't understand, I'm trying to let go' or 'Easy for you to say "relax", you're not the one going through this!'

The concept of **not** fighting against our situations and ourselves can seem counterproductive, yet it's in this state that we can find pure flow and true empowerment. In this state, we're able to take a step back and see a higher perspective. We're able to feel our way through life, instead of trying to think our way out of things.

❦ Instead of fighting, you can surrender ❧

Instead of struggling, you can flow. Instead of harassing your-self and being hard on yourself, instead of rooting yourself in the cause of an issue, you can actually let it go.

I know this because I've had to do it, and because I know it can feel so hard to do. Yet I also know it's possible and necessary and healing. Letting go is deeply healing. Holding on keeps us rooted in time and it's in this space that we're not accomplishing, we're not achieving. We're growing roots into ground we don't want to be connected to. Holding on and being rooted in negativity is not the same as being grounded in a sense of self. We're creating a forest of unwelcome and unwanted thoughts, and it becomes so thick and entangled we can't even find our way out of it.

We think if we surrender we won't get what we want, but so often the universe brings back to us what we desire in beautiful, unexpected ways. And while this may not be on **our** time, it's on Divine time. And remember, Divine time is always on time.

Here's an affirmation you may like to repeat to yourself or record as a mini guided meditation, or perhaps even write it out and stick it somewhere where you'll see it every single day.

❦ The Go with the Flow Affirmation ❧

I surrender.

I let go.

I trust I'm exactly where I'm supposed to be.

I know that trusting this will allow me to feel more connected, guided, supported and grounded, and I know I'm being guided on my current path because this is the right path for me to be on.

I'm aligned to my growth and transformation in whichever way betters me for my highest good. I let go of all that no longer serves me. It's safe for me to let things be easy. It's easy for me to let things go with the flow.

I love and forgive myself.

I surrender. I let go. I know I'm exactly where I'm supposed to be.

I allow the flow to take me where I need to go.

I surrender.

I let go.

Say this affirmation to yourself each morning and night, for as long as feels good to you. You may choose to write down some reflections about how you're feeling before, or free write in your journal afterwards. Whatever comes up is perfect for you, and will be healing on some level (and sometimes on more than one level).

Chapter 13

do you accept yourself?

୧୨ୗ୨୭

Because if we all waited ... waited and waited until we were shiny and bright and new, not one of us on the planet could bear to love ourselves. And without that love, that deep centered source of life ... without that love we are doomed to keep flailing, keep lashing out, keep damaging others with our wounds, keep on keeping on with being unconscious. And so somehow ... love must lead the way ...

Leonie Dawson

I used to find it so hard to accept myself and—those scary words—love myself. Even just the concept of self-acceptance seemed completely foreign to me, whether it was in relation to parts of my personality, my situation, and especially when it came to my body. I couldn't understand how people could be happy with their bodies unless they were thin and fit and radiating health (in fact, I believed you could only radiate health if you **were** thin).

I didn't believe I could accept myself until I approved of myself. And I didn't trust myself to approve of myself as I was, lest that meant I stopped trying to grow and advance, lose weight, get healthier, slim down and tone up.

I remember how much it grated against me when someone said, 'Just accept yourself, accept your situation' or especially something like, 'Accept your body.' I used to think that meant I would never do better, if I was only accepting myself for who I was and not for who I wanted to be, or who I knew I could be. I didn't want to accept myself, as didn't that mean accepting defeat or cementing my fate and keeping myself stuck where I was? How could **acceptance** ever allow me to be happier or more accomplished? No, not for me, thank you.

And if my constant comparison was an indication that I wasn't good enough, how in the world was self-acceptance going to allow me to create the things I wanted in my life? If acceptance meant being okay with how things were, did that also mean I wasn't ever going to improve?

If there's one thing that frightens a perfectionist, it's the idea of never getting better at something. Yet in reality, it's this lack of self-acceptance that's truly keeping us stuck.

When you don't accept yourself, no matter where you are or how far you've come, you're pressing pause on the story of your life. You'll find yourself stuck in self-perpetuating patterns, because to leave these patterns behind, to find the light that sits quietly beneath the darkness of your lack of faith in yourself, takes some work and love and care.

The work isn't in the pushing; it's in the accepting.

The shift to self-acceptance isn't in telling yourself you'll never be good enough; it's in being brave enough to say you're good enough for self-acceptance, today.

And honestly, I know this can all feel like a lot of work. It can feel hard and you can feel so down in the dumps about what you're going through, and yet it's your choice.

At the end of the day, self-acceptance is a choice you make, every day. Like self-worth, no-one can give it to you or take it away from you. I can't make the decision for you; neither can your partner or your parents or your best friend. You can seek support from therapists, you can go to daily yoga classes, you can journal and meditate and drink green juice daily. You can do all of these wonderful things which will help you on so many levels, but self-acceptance doesn't come just because of the things you do. It doesn't come just because you bought a new journal or finally did a headstand in your yoga practice, or because you cut out coffee this week.

You might fool yourself for a little while looking just at the external things you're adding into your life which make you feel more accepting of yourself. But the truth is that you can accept yourself no matter where you are, what you're doing, or what colour your morning juice is. (As a funny aside, one of my yoga teachers calls coffee 'black juice' ... yes, that's one of my favourite kinds of juices!)

As you start to find it easier and more natural to accept yourself today, you'll be called to not only look at your present moment but also your past.

⟪ True acceptance of the past and present ⟫

Not accepting yourself may be affecting your desire to improve, progress and grow. The more you struggle and fight with yourself, forcing yourself to accept yourself, the less acceptance you really feel.

Is there something you're finding hard to accept in your life? What are you not accepting of yourself, and how is this affecting your ability to release comparison and elevate your thoughts and energy?

True self-acceptance is about releasing any guilt you may be holding onto for not being who you think you should be, or for falling short of your desired goals or outcomes.

Accepting yourself is being comfortable with who you are—perceived deficiencies, transgressions, flaws and all. To accept yourself, you must surrender and let go of any perceptions of your flaws, past or present.

Self-acceptance allows you to love all parts of yourself, and honour yourself. When you can do this, then self-comparison is able to fall away with ease. It stops being a constant in your life, because you genuinely celebrate who you are, what you're doing and where you're going.

You will start to know that you don't need to compare yourself to your past or future self, or to someone else, because you wholly accept where you are and who you are.

᚛ Perfectionism and self-acceptance ᚜

Answer these questions honestly:

- Do you think being a perfectionist (or wanting things to be a certain way, all the time with no exception) is allowing you to accept yourself today?
- Or is this keeping your focus on the future only, with the flimsy promise of self-acceptance, when you're better, smarter, wealthier, healthier, thinner, braver or more successful?

So many of my clients are perfectionists too. I remember one session in which my client sat in front of me, looking at me through teary, worried eyes. 'I'm a perfectionist; it's the only way I know how to do things,' she said. We were talking about life, food, exercise and work. So many aspects of her life were merging into one lump of chronic dissatisfaction, because she was being so incredibly hard on herself.

She knew exactly what she was putting herself through, because she'd done it before. And she was admitting to herself that she'd keep doing it, if she didn't start to release these negative patterns and limiting mindsets.

She wanted to stop, and she knew it would come down to her mindset. She knew she had to forgive herself, in order to accept herself. She knew she had to start being softer, in order to step forwards. She knew all of this; now she had to give herself permission to do it, and let go of her fears around never being enough. Because when you can let go of these fears, you'll see you're already enough, and in fact, you always have been.

Discovering how to start accepting yourself and then truly accepting yourself is about not only releasing perceived flaws and letting go of old mistakes, but also about being kinder and gentler to yourself, and even embracing the side of you that does its best to make you push yourself harder.

There are so many reasons why being a perfectionist isn't helping you become a more loving, accepting, truth-seeking version of yourself. There are so many reasons why being a perfectionist is making you feel stuck in your life, as if no matter when or how you surrendered to your forceful ways (if you even knew how to do that) no good could come of it anyway.

I know all of this because I could be the biggest perfectionist if I let myself get stuck in that mindset. It's something I've learnt to work with through working on myself, and through working with my clients, helping them to be softer with themselves.

There's nothing wrong with wanting the very best for yourself, but being a perfectionist doesn't always mean you create the very best for yourself, does it? The version in your head is always different to how events and situations transpire and you're often left feeling empty and defeated, as if you didn't try hard enough, like you could've done more if you'd simply **been** more.

Fear of failure can show up in many ways in our lives, and procrastination is one of them. As a perfectionist, it's so much easier to simply not do something than to do it, but tell yourself it's not good enough and never will be. Over the years, I've worked on this side of myself so that I could release it. Momentum is my modus operandi and I love it. I would rather write something, edit it until it feels right, then release it into the world knowing I can always improve it, but not letting that notion stop me from doing the work today. The masterpiece of your life must be released. After reading Todd Henry's book, *Die Empty*, I know that I don't want to die with my best work inside me. And if that means releasing something that isn't perfect, but is still the very best I could do with what I had and what I knew, then I'll do that every time.

Is this the same for you; or is your perfectionism and lack of self-acceptance stopping you from doing something?

Take it from me … if you just take the first step to beginning whatever it is you're holding in your heart (whether it's stepping into acceptance, creating something, releasing something or someone from your life, or has something to do with work or your home life), you'll soon see how brave and willing and courageous you're being. And this will fuel you to keep going.

Don't distract yourself with perfectionism. How boring. You have so much more to give, to love, to extend, to offer, to create and most importantly, to release. Don't let your perfectionism stop you from starting. Don't let it stop you from starting to accept yourself, from surrendering and letting go, from releasing your fears or from being kinder to yourself.

Your perfectionism might just be a drop in the ocean of your self-acceptance, but it's an important drop, and it reaches every other drop in the ocean of your life.

Even though you might wish to pile other labels on top of this (call it self-improvement or not starting until you're ready), the truth is you are ready to accept yourself, today.

And once you give yourself this permission, things will start to fall into place, and this will allow you to feel even more supported by yourself.

❧ Celebration vs. self-beration ❧

Just like perfectionism, we can berate ourselves and give ourselves such a hard time, whether or not we label this perfectionism. Sometimes it's just pure, cold criticism, and it's not always constructive.

Sometimes we think we have forever to improve ourselves. We don't realise how much time we lose by not being happy with who we are, because we don't think we're good enough to earn our own approval. If we never celebrate ourselves because we think we have eternity to keep improving, then we'll leave this world having never enjoyed our own company, our own achievements, growth and progress. We'll consistently push ourselves to breaking point, berating ourselves and never enjoying what we're creating for ourselves.

Start celebrating who you are, today

Whatever you're doing, stop for a moment (except reading. Keep reading). Take a look around you, at your life, at yourself. What have you achieved that you never thought possible? What would last year's version of you say, if they saw where you are today? Are you acknowledging your progress, achievements and growth?

We're given a new chance to love and accept ourselves each time we open our eyes to a new day. If that means you have to take a nap to start the day again, by all means … go right ahead.

We're given a new chance to love and accept ourselves each time we take a new breath. If that means walking out of a meeting to take some new deep breaths, or meditating three times a day, or starting and ending your day with a run, a yoga class, or even a cleansing scream or cry (maybe not every day, but when you need to) then please, take that opportunity.

The person you were yesterday has created the person you are today, and that person has done a pretty awesome job.

Sure you can keep upgrading your life, but if you're not celebrating yourself, then you'll never notice the new scenery.

Be compassionate to yourself. Forgive yourself for past wrongdoings or shortcomings. Release any guilt you're holding on to about the way you think things should have turned out, things you think you should have said or places you should or shouldn't have gone.

What would it truly take for you to start celebrating who you are, right now? Would you have to lose more weight first? Or launch your new website? Would you have to earn more money, or find a new loving partner? Would you have to buy a bigger house or sell your things and finally move overseas?

Now think of doing all of those things from a space of self-acceptance. Think of eating clean, healthy food from an energy that helps you feel uplifted and supported, instead of criticised and resentful.

Think of starting your business or taking it to the next level from a space of pride, holding your head high and knowing you're doing your best every single day. How much easier would your world be if you **started** with self-acceptance? How much further could you travel, how much higher could you fly, and how much deeper could you go, if self-acceptance was part of your everyday world?

I can tell you from my experience that self-acceptance helped me feel so much more confident about who I am. It helped me get off the 'yoyo' dieting bandwagon I was on in my early twenties. It helped me stop overexercising and controlling every forkful of food I let myself eat.

And here's another bright spark of truth to light your way forward: you don't need to wait to celebrate. You can start today.

Once you can start to accept that daily celebration of who you are is important and necessary in releasing yourself from the comparison trap, you can take steps to really incorporate this into your world.

So often, we wait to celebrate ourselves. We wait to accept ourselves, and to say we've done enough. We wait for 'one day', every day. And of course it never comes, because we're always waiting for it.

How can you celebrate yourself today? Perhaps through something you do for yourself, like indulging in a massage to celebrate a huge week at work, or buying yourself a bunch of flowers for making headway in a project, or simply taking a few hours out of your busy schedule to rest and restore yourself. How can you celebrate today?

Chapter 14

forgiveness, truth and integrity

⤳⤳⤳

e've discussed surrendering, and now I'm going to ask you to put this notion into practice in a similar way. Is there something you're holding on to, whether it's an experience or a current situation, or even a standard you've held yourself to for ages, that's just not working for you? It's time to forgive yourself for it.

Forgiveness doesn't mean failure. Forgiveness doesn't mean you're compromising your strength or integrity. Forgiveness means you're stronger than you thought you were. It means you're able to rise above and see a higher perspective, see that the best way to create your best life is to let go of what you're holding on to.

I used to hold on to the concept that I was always bigger than my friends, and that I would never be happy in my body. I used to consistently berate myself and give myself a hard time about my weight, the food I was eating or not eating, how often I went to gym and how hard I worked out. I used to carry so much anger and resentment that I remember a time when I wished an illness or injury upon myself, so I might lose weight in hospital, without having to try so hard for it. Seriously. (Yeah, I know how that sounds, by the way!)

There came a day (or rather many days, one by one, step by step, moment by moment) when I consciously started to forgive myself and let it go. I couldn't change the past, what had happened to me or how I'd felt for years. But I could ensure I went forward with a new mindset, and a new energy. And the only person who could give me permission to do that was myself.

Get to know yourself

Part of embracing self-acceptance is discovering who you truly are, and what lights you up. For instance, I've mentioned I used to sometimes force myself to go to bars and nightclubs when I was younger, because I thought I had to. All my friends were doing it, in fact they loved it. And while there was a stage where I did find elements of it enjoyable, it wasn't really satisfying for me and it never quite fitted with me. Even if I went out with close friends, I felt like I had to force myself to make conversation and smile a lot, always shouting over the music and trying to look like I was having a great time. I always felt the biggest, sweetest rush of relief as I slipped out the club and into a taxi home.

Part of my journey to self-acceptance was voicing my likes and dislikes, not just to myself, but to the people in my life too. It's now almost a joke between me and some of my friends that if an arrangement involves a nightclub, you just know I won't be there. Now I'm okay with it, and so are my friends.

I remember another occasion when I was called to really accept a part of myself that some people in my life didn't want to. I was on a weekend away with my hubby, after a few busy and intense weeks. For me, winding down on a weekend with a glass of red wine, some great food and a decluttered calendar makes me swoon with happiness. I posted something on my private social media page about our weekend plans, which included not much more than relaxing, drinking coffee and wine, and reading, plus there was this gorgeous old-fashioned claw foot bath that had my name all over it. On the first night there, I ran a hot bath and hopped in with a big glass of red and a new novel. Heaven, right?

An old schoolfriend made a slightly scathing comment about how that would be her version of a nightmare weekend. She intimated she'd much prefer to be out drinking and blowing off steam that way. I laughed it off, while at the same time accepting that her version of relaxing is so very different to mine, and that's more than okay. To be honest, after a hugely busy time at work, if I'd had to go out socialising, drinking and burning off steam, I'd have burnt myself to a crisp and left not much of me behind.

I know this about myself; I need to create time and space around me in order to recover, and I replenish my energy on my own or when I'm with a small group of people I love. Sending me out to a nightclub when I'm tired is like sending a weary soldier onto the battlefield again. Except this time, it's my energetic boundaries that get injured.

Getting to know yourself and embracing what you find puts you on the straight and narrow to self-acceptance. When you accept yourself, you open doors to all the good stuff you'd miss if you kept charging onwards, striving for your worth and for the validation of others.

✎ Tell yourself the truth ✎

What if you trusted yourself enough to tell yourself the truth about who you are, what you need, and why you can start accepting yourself right now?

I have a post-it on my wall behind my computer (yes, I have many post-its on this wall!) and this quote jumps out at me as I think about trust. It's from author and entrepreneur Seth Godin, who says: *When in doubt, tell yourself the truth.*

It's such a simple premise, right? And it sounds counterintuitive. But as soon as you embrace this idea, amazing things can happen for you.

The honest truth might mean you admit that you're being really hard on yourself, and that when you're comparing yourself to someone else you're really saying, 'I want that too; how can I make this happen for me?'

The truth might mean you admit that you're ready to allow yourself to be kinder and gentler to yourself, or that even though you're pushing so hard, a part of you really does feel like you're in the right place in your life.

The honest truth might mean admitting that, even though you didn't get what you want, you got something even better. It means knowing you're worthy of accepting yourself today, before you've gotten out of bed, answered emails or had a green smoothie. And afterwards, when you're making breakfast or tea or grabbing a coffee before your day begins.

The honest truth is that you're worthy, no matter what those fear-based, ego-ridden thoughts are telling you. Our fear is often telling us the opposite of what is true. (Of course this isn't always the case; when your fear says, *Please don't walk down that dark street*, trust it!)

Sometimes it's hard to discern what the difference is between fear that's saying *Back away* or *Don't say 'yes' to this* and fear that's actually expansive, the kind of fear that means taking a risk could really pay off. The latter kind of fear or resistance could lead you to an even greater truth about yourself, could expand your energy and raise you to greater heights in your life.

In a kinesiology balance, I'll use muscle testing to ascertain a percentage of the client's stress or contraction, and their life energy or expansion in relation to their goal. There's a wonderful little activity you can do right now to help you work out if you're feeling contracted or expansive, in relation to something that's going on for you. Take a few deep breaths. Spend a moment or two simply tuning in to your body's own messages and energy. Think about the goal or your desire.

Does your body and energy feel open, expansive, light and free? That's a big **'yes'**. Or does your body and energy feel stuck, contracted, stagnant, panicky? That's a **'no'**.

ꙮ Start today ꙮ

No more waiting for acceptance and celebration, remember? If there's one thing you do when you finish reading this chapter, I'd like it to be that you start loving yourself and accepting yourself for the beautiful human you are.

Even if there's an area of your life that feels uncomfortable and isn't currently fully aligned with who you are, or where you see yourself, it doesn't mean you aren't worthy of your own acceptance, or your own compassion or gentleness.

No matter what you're going through in your life, you're worthy of self-acceptance. No matter how much you're constantly comparing yourself to others, you're still amazing. You still wake up every day and put your best foot forward, even if some days it feels like you're taking leaps backwards. You are leaping forwards, every single day. Now you just need to acknowledge it, treasure yourself, accept yourself, and be a witness to yourself.

There is so much we can learn from ourselves when we are open and willing. When we give ourselves not only the chance to get to know ourselves, but permission to change, to grow, to invest our energy into accepting ourselves, rather than judging ourselves.

Part Three

intuition, wisdom, guidance

Chapter 15

the pillars of connection, clarity, guidance and grace

༄ঞ༄

There's a process I take myself through when I feel I need a little extra guidance and clarity. It usually begins with me sitting down at my desk, on our couch or ottoman or anywhere quiet, somewhere that feels light and open, somewhere that's vibrating at just the right frequency for where I feel I'm at. I pull out my notebook or journal. I settle into my skin, my body, my breath, my energy. It's my intent to connect, to shut out and close down anything else that's on and hovering in my peripheral vision, to ignore emails and texts and notifications, to honour myself, my time, my Divine grace and my energy.

So once I am sitting down I do whatever I need to do to deepen this connection; I might journal, meditate, pull an oracle card, take an energetic essence or oil or use a spray. Then I gather this energy inside and I start listening to what comes through, to what needs to be processed and integrated; but mostly, I trust. I trust that what I receive is right. I then focus my attention and energy on what needs to be released … in order to receive.

This process has a few stages, and so here they are for you to work with … my five pillars of Divine connection, clarity, guidance and grace. I hope you'll take them with you on your journey to abundant self-worth and internal validation.

Pillar One: Connecting

The first pillar is about simply connecting to something other than your conscious, everyday, all-consuming thoughts. Sometimes this means disconnecting, but to disconnect from those thoughts means you've opened a new channel of higher power, higher being, higher love and authenticity.

Initially, disconnecting might mean you distract yourself from comparison and low self-worth with something shiny and not really helpful (like TV, the internet, or that funny video about fainting goats! Look it up, but not right now).

I'm asking you to go a little deeper here. I'm asking you to commit to connection. When was the last time you just sat with yourself? I don't even mean in meditation, yoga or journaling … but the last time you just sat with yourself, and committed to drown out the noise with a deeper, higher knowledge.

Connecting to your inner guide, your intuition, your inner compass, wisdom or guidance is impossible if you don't ask to connect to it. So, take a deep breath and ask.

✌ Pillar Two: Deepening ☙

This is about deepening the connection you've been building in order to find the clarity you're seeking; it's about investing in your intuition and the connection you've built, keeping the faith, your knowing and knowledge.

This is more than just making time to go to yoga each week (although that's so helpful and beautiful). This is about deepening your connection with yourself, and diving down so you can open up to higher guidance. When I think of deepening my spirituality, I think of honouring myself and what I need. I think back to the times I had to 'unfollow' people on social media, because I wasn't in the headspace to witness their lives and not feel threatened or compare myself to them. I did this while extending love and compassion to them, and in doing so, I extended more love and compassion to myself too.

This space allowed me to deepen my connection to myself. I blocked out what needed blocking out (at the time). I opened up to what I needed, in order to reconnect and reconstruct the parts I was losing to fear, to lack, to fighting and struggle. Once I did this, I could see it had been the right thing for me at the time and, most importantly, it allowed me to fill a hole inside that I'd been trying to fill, by comparing myself and pushing myself to perfectionism. After a while, I didn't need to keep my door to the world closed anymore, and you don't have to either.

Deepening your connection to wisdom and guidance isn't about drowning out the noise of your ego or closing yourself off; it's about your resolving to reveal the depths of yourself, so you can fill the cracks with the light you crave. It's about carving out your special space in this world … the space that has your name written all over it, if only you'd dare to look over and see it.

ﷻ Pillar Three: Trusting ﷻ

This is when we start truly trusting ourselves and our guidance, as well as the timing of our lives. We become effortlessly patient and committed to our own path, because we know this is the best way to be.

My very favourite quote for the past almost-fifteen years is by the late Wayne Dyer, who said: *Everything is perfect in the universe, even your desire to improve it.*

For many reasons, this quote tells us to **trust**. From the day I first heard that quote, it has calmed my soul at the deepest level. It's like a cooling, healing balm on a patch of hot, sunburned skin.

It says trust. Trust. Trust.

Trust the timing of your life. Trust yourself and your intuition. Even if these messages feel daunting, trust them to guide you to where you need to be. Trust them to be your compass. Trust them to hold your hand when you say, 'Life, I want to show up. I want to meet you halfway; will you be there when I arrive?' And then show up. Fully. Completely. Committed. Trusting.

Pillar Four: Releasing

By the time you've energetically reached and embraced this pillar, you're ready to release what needs to be set free. Whether it's your comparing ways, your fears, or your mistrust of the universe or yourself, you're ready to integrate all you've learnt, to complete this for what it needs to show you, to let go, to let go, to let go.

This may come in the form of lengthy, juicy journaling sessions, of soulful chats with yourself in a park on a sunny afternoon, of deep yoga poses that release tension and tightness and fears from your hips, your heart, your mind.

Or perhaps it comes in the form of full moon meditations, workshops, breathing, or investing energy where you finally feel it can go. Freedom and harmony come from forgiveness, releasing and letting go.

Pillar Five: Receiving

At the end of this process, you're ready to fully let go to come up full again, and from this space you'll see that you're ready to start receiving what you ask for ... or something better.

This is when synchronicity starts to flow through our life. This is when we hear true and authentic guidance and follow its lead. This is when new ideas, phrases and whole sentences download into our consciousness and we stop mid-stir while cooking our morning oats and grab the nearest notebook to scribble down words of wisdom. It's wisdom that comes through us and yet it's not always made of us. This is the grace and wisdom we want to channel, to bottle, to receive, to allow in. This is the grace and wisdom that'll whisper: *You're worthy, you're good enough, and you've got this, go this way* … when your path feels cluttered, clumpy and stuck.

This guidance is received when we're ready, when our energy is clear and aligned, when we're open to it. This guidance is received when we've cut ties we no longer need; the ties that hold us back and make us feel crushed, like we'll never be good enough because someone else has what we want. These ties keep us locked in lack, and it's in this state of lack that we compare and criticise ourselves even more.

Open the channels that run through you. Cut the ties that hold you back. Clear, calm and align yourself to receive the abundance that's available to you, and to receive the wisdom that is your birthright. Gather up the guidance, the support, the healing and the intuitive manifestation that is within you and within your grasp. Claim it as your own because, in all honesty, it is your own. And you're the only one who could ever say it's not.

ᥱᥬ Sweet and subtle ᦄᦉ

When worked with from a space of openness, compassion and forgiveness, these five pillars will allow you to increase your self-confidence. Your worth is already inside you but you'll feel it even more deeply. You'll be able to stand up more easily, to feel guided by your own wisdom and knowledge and to not only release comparison but to be truly happy for the object of your envy or jealousy.

Remember, we're being taught a lesson when we feel envious or jealous. We can use it, or lose it. It's our choice. It doesn't have to be a huge, scarring and jarring lesson; it can be sweet and subtle. It can soften the edges of our consciousness so we're able to expand into a higher plane, deepening our roots and spreading our wings. It can be what we need it to be when we're in the right place to take what we need, release what we don't, and feel grateful and compassionate for the whole hot mess.

All of this will increase your ability to monitor your comparison scale and cut ties when they need cutting. Energetically, when you compare you're tying yourself to someone else's success and energy, and your guidance channels become confused. You're no longer completely in your own energy. How can you be your best self when you're energetically tied to someone else, and feeling pulled down and held back because of it?

The scenic route

When we never give ourselves a break from constant comparison and criticism, we also block ourselves from listening to our intuition, wisdom and guidance. We worry that we've fallen off our path and, although we can see the well-trodden path of whoever we've put on a pedestal, we've blocked ourselves from seeing our own. We think our path could never be good enough anyway, but we still want to see a way forward.

We forget to use reasoning. That person's path is their path because of everything that's happened in their life up until that point: where they were born, who their parents are, what school they went to, whether they studied at university or not, their traits and personality, their own dreams and desires and goals. You can't have what they have in its exact form because you are who you are, and that's how you're supposed to be. Part of removing yourself from the comparison trap is about letting go of others' paths and focusing solely, wholly and completely on your own.

And one of the loveliest ways to do this, so you feel grounded, connected and full of faith, is to start by truly trusting in the universe and your path in life, so you know you're heading in the right direction.

Sometimes this direction takes us through scenery we never thought we'd see, and sometimes we can't see the bigger picture. I've been there too; through times when I thought I was on the most perfect path, only to have the path pulled out from under me, like Aladdin and his magic carpet. That's okay; when you feel aligned with who you are and where you're going, not seeing the bigger picture can actually still feel safe.

Can you think of any times in your life where something that initially seemed difficult or troublesome turned into something really positive for you?

This is your guidance. Maybe you didn't listen to the whispers of your inner wisdom and so the universe had to speak up a little louder to get your attention. You don't need to let it shout at you again, you can listen to it closely and be in tune with where you're being guided. You can build your inner intuition compass to guide you and protect you.

Chapter 16

connecting to your inner guide

ℳℴℳ

o you ever feel that you're blocking yourself from listening to your inner guide? Your inner guide wants to show you how to find freedom, and your inner critic wants to keep you where you are. Your inner guide knows how to unblock yourself from listening to your inner critic. Yet your inner critic tells you you're not worthy of the confidence you could unleash if you truly listened.

Let me ask you a question: Is there any part of you that believes you'll be able to truly follow your own guidance and path if you're always stuck in comparison, in fight or flight mode?

If you find it really hard to listen to your inner guide and be led down a path that feels right for you, then it makes total sense that your confidence, sense of self, purpose and self-worth would feel a little unaligned.

When you constantly compare yourself to other people, you're in fact creating disharmony with your own goals, dreams and self-worth, in relation to achieving these things.

In the flow

Eyes bright, heart open, mind clear. That's how you can feel when you're in the flow with the universe, when you feel aligned and clear, when your confidence is sky-high and you feel as though you're manifesting everything you desire.

Yet what happens when we're not in the flow, when we feel stuck, when we feel blocked, when we feel like things just aren't working for us? When I was struggling to connect with my inner compass and direct myself out of comparison, I did feel like I was blocking myself and knew I was getting in my own way. It came down to fear. How scared was I of not doing the right thing? How scared was I of actually becoming successful? Was I up for the challenge? Did I want to draw attention to myself, to become visible? Did I have the confidence to lead, and to make big, bold decisions?

Fear blocks us from listening to our deepest intuition, the part of us that knows we could be doing things differently, or the part of us that wants to shed old layers and start afresh. Yet the more you begin to connect with your guidance and intuition, the sooner you'll build up your self-belief and self-confidence and find the clarity you're craving. You'll also realise your fear is just trying to keep you safe, and that while you can acknowledge its presence, it doesn't need to define you or your actions.

Your wisdom is older than you

They say we become wiser when we let go of what we no longer need. Our wisdom is carried in us through lifetimes. I'm sure you've experienced that feeling of meeting an 'old soul'. I believe that some of us carry more wisdom than others, or perhaps are just more in tune with it. I've come across people in my life who I feel are very young at a soul level; they're like excited puppies. They make many mistakes in life and they bounce back; they don't always learn their lessons quickly but they often leave their mark.

For you to feel deeply worthy, you must recognise that your wisdom is older than this lifetime, it's older than the version of you that you know today. Your inner wisdom can guide you, helping you to uncover what needs shedding and showing you the way forward.

Don't be afraid of this wisdom. Over the years I've witnessed so many of my clients who feel incredibly in tune with themselves, but fear their own wisdom. They've hidden behind it, or downplayed it with their friends and family. They fear they'll be judged or laughed at.

We don't need to hide from our wisdom; we need to open ourselves to it, face up, eyes bright, hearts open.

A little while ago I had dinner with some old friends and somehow the topic turned to energetic healing. Next to writing, I feel deeply that energetic and emotional healing is my purpose (combine them and you have my version of heaven on earth). So when this came up with a group of friends who don't usually talk much about spirituality or energetics, I got quite excited. Not all of their reactions to the conversation were positive, and this was completely their own experience and context. That might have upset me when I started on my kinesiology journey, several years before this particular dinner. Back then I may have tried to talk them into understanding it, or seeing it the way I do. But I accepted the conversation for what it was; I didn't need to teach my friends anything; we all learn what we need to, when we need it.

Our level of connection to our wisdom is only as deep as it needs to be for the lessons we're learning right now. You can deepen your connection to your inner wisdom when you're ready. Sometimes you can tell the universe when this is, and sometimes you'll be told when the time is right. It's all a process of integration, learning, clearing, balancing and healing.

When the time is right, you'll feel it, across all layers of yourself and your being, through every cell, in every corner of your being. Your higher self will be calling out to listen and you'll turn your face up, gladly.

Here's a little inner guide affirmation you may want to work with:

*I'm ready and open to receive insight from my inner guide.
I welcome these insights, this guidance, this direction, and
I'm ready to accept this support.*

*I know I'm worthy of listening, of hearing, of being
guided and supported, knowing that when I feel more
grounded and at ease, I'm able to fully empower myself on
a very deep level.*

*I know I'm on the right path, I know it's now safe for
me to truly listen to my higher self, my guidance and my
wisdom, knowing this comes naturally to me, knowing I'm
worthy of this.*

Chapter 17

connecting to your higher self

❧

little while ago I lay down for a guided meditation by Sonia Choquette (a fellow Hay House author), where I was to meet my higher self. I felt a little nervous, but mostly excited and open.

Sonia guided me to lift up out of my body and look down at my physical body below me. I began to visualise this, and to meet my higher self. I can't explain what my higher self looked like or sounded like, except that she was so energetic. She was happy and she laughed a lot. She just kept saying to me, 'It's amazing! It's all going to be amazing! Stop worrying, stop worrying, stop worrying!' Then she would giggle, and move around her space a lot. At the end of the meditation I felt so calm and serene. I knew in my heart that my higher self was so chilled out about where I was going and how I was getting there, and that I could listen to her and trust her.

You can also meet your higher self, whether it's through a regular meditation practice, a guided meditation or session with a healer, or anything else that resonates with you. Connecting to your higher self will allow you to see the truth of your situation, whether it's that you're always loved, supported and worthy, or that you're on the right path and going well.

I truthfully believe that whatever you're doing right now is perfect for you. It's what you're supposed to be doing, and it's where you're supposed to be. When you connect with your higher self, you'll believe that too.

You'll see you don't need to compare yourself to anyone else. You'll know you're already a container for so much innate value and self-worth. Your higher self knows you are exactly who you're supposed to be, doing what you're supposed to be doing. If you listen, you'll hear this. Then you can choose to believe and accept it too.

Here's an affirmation you may want to use to call in guidance from your higher self:

I choose to welcome in guidance from my higher self now.
I make space for new insights and guidance to drop in.
I know whatever comes through is safe for me to listen to
and act on, and I trust this guidance will help me move
forwards and claim my own power and inner strength.
I am worthy of this guidance and I am empowered by it.

Remember to use this affirmation in any way that works for you. You could also simplify it and add a daily reminder to your phone that says: *I'm worthy, I'm guided, I'm supported and I'm loved.* You'll be amazed by how many times this pops up at the perfect moment.

Chapter 18

divine timing and that thing called patience

⚜

hroughout my years of working with clients, I think I've only had a handful who've sat down in front of me and said they feel they are patient people. Mostly, we joke together, 'Oh yeah, sure, I'm patient. I'm pretty chilled. I can wait. Just call me Miss Patient!'

I know this feeling of needing to rush and craving the speed and satisfaction that comes with movement and momentum all too well, because I'm also not the world's most patient human. But, I trust in Divine timing.

The Divine timing of your life is a puzzle that doesn't come with the finished product displayed proudly on the outside of the box. You must be okay (more than okay!) with trusting the timing of your life. The more you search for the image of the whole puzzle, the less you're likely to see the image of your highest self and truest purpose in your reflection.

And remember, your highest self is the highest vibration of your potential; it carries the wisdom you need to release comparison, to feel into your worth, to know you're on the right track.

Why rush things? If a puzzle piece falls into your lap and you're not ready, you won't even be aware it's a piece of the puzzle, because you don't need it yet. We need to trust that the puzzle pieces will fall into our lap when we're ready for them, and not a moment sooner.

We can laugh at how much we want things **now** but that won't change a thing. Even if we rush, we still have to wait, and playing the waiting game feels awful. What if we didn't feel like we had to wait but instead we could just **be**? How much better would it be to slip into a comfortable state of being present, of being open, of letting ourselves trust and have faith, rather than waiting, waiting, and waiting?

Waiting causes anxiety and restlessness. It thumps in our heart like a thousand butterflies demanding to be let out. Trusting and keeping the faith are side effects of patience, and patience is what'll help you feel complete, resolved and on the right path, before the object of your desire has even arrived in your life.

Your purpose isn't to wait; it's to be. To be here now, to be here fully. It's to know your worth, your value, and yourself. It's to honour, protect and work with this in order to fulfil your higher purpose and bring out the very best of yourself, every single day.

Chapter 19

synchronicity and confirmation

♈

When I started practising as a nutritionist and naturopath, I always loved focusing on the emotional aspects of whatever was going on for my clients. Several years later, when I added kinesiology to my practice, within a month I was so fully booked that clients had to wait up to six or eight weeks for a session. I was humbled and grateful, and I knew why this was so. It's because we want to know we're on the right track, doing the right thing, and aligned with our potential, ensuring we're getting closer to where we see ourselves in our future. And kinesiology, energetic healing and balancing allows us to get closer to this; it allows us to find a sense of flow and synchronicity in our lives. When we're flowing, we're so much more at ease. It brings forth confirmation of what we need to let go of, where we can best direct our energy and how to make the most of where we are, without needing to be more or have more.

When we feel off track, that's when life feels like a bit of a struggle. We may get overwhelmed by even the smallest task or add too much to our plates, and then berate ourselves when we don't complete everything we set out to do that day or week.

Sometimes our intuition connects head-on with synchronicity and leads to incredible things happening. In fact, you could say it was my inner guide who introduced me to the man who is now my husband, Nic.

I woke up one Saturday morning, several years ago, with the realisation I had to leave the four-year relationship I'd been in. Four days later, I went to an event where I met Nic. We started dating the next month and two years later he smashed a glass with his foot (the Jewish way of saying 'I do').

My inner guide woke me up on that Saturday morning and told me my fear of the unknown was only as bad as I imagined it to be. Wasn't it better to try a new vision out for size than stay where I was, fearing a future I would never have because I was too scared to go out and meet it?

ལྕ Confirmation and clarity ৩৲

As a society, we crave confirmation. The future is where we project our fears, so it feels uncertain and scary sometimes. We project our anxieties into the future and lose our connection with today. We fail to acknowledge how well we're doing right now, and worry until we feel sick with inner turmoil.

You can find synchronicity in your daily life, when you're aligned to yourself on a very deep level. I want you to start noticing where there is synchronicity and flow in your life, and feel aligned to bringing in incredible amounts of joy, happiness, success and confidence.

You'll be reminded

Even as I write this, I am reminded how the universe supports, guides and reminds us on our path in life. As a kinesiologist, I will often do mini alignments or balances on myself, where I will align myself with a goal and then clear away any stress that pops up.

I did one recently when I was midway through writing a different chapter. A little niggling doubt had popped up and I wasn't sure if I was heading in the right direction with it. So I sat myself down and typed out some goals I wanted to clear stress on and align myself to. Here are some of the goals I created for myself:

- I let my writing be easy for me.
- I trust I'm writing what will resonate with my readers.
- I'm open to letting my book develop over time.
- I know I'm on the right track with my book and my writing.

Using muscle testing, I then asked my body what was blocking me from aligning to those goals, and was guided to pull a card from Doreen Virtue's *Life Purpose Oracle Card Deck.* Incredibly, the card that fell out was ... *Writing: you heal, inspire, teach and entertain with the words you write.* I burst out laughing. Hello universe! Hello sweet synchronicity! Hello beautiful, glorious confirmation.

If ever I was looking for confirmation that I was writing the **right** thing, then I had found it. Or rather, it had found me!

This happens to my clients all the time. They come in for a session with an open heart, and their body and the universe guides them to find the information, the signs, the confirmation they need.

Think with your heart

We crave synchronicity and guidance, and we can find it in our everyday lives, through listening to our own guidance and intuition, and then ensuring we're open to receiving it.

I recently saw a client who was craving confirmation. She had just gone through a major restructure at work and her job had been very up in the air for a while. She had taken on much more than she could handle in her professional life and was managing several huge projects all at once. By the time she came to see me for a session, she had a lot of processing and integrating to do with many lessons learnt over previous months, yet she couldn't see her way out of the harder months to come. She craved confirmation that she was making the right decisions and doing the right things.

There were incredible synchronicities that came up for her throughout the session, and by the end she felt at peace with where she was in her life. To close our session we pulled a card for her and, as I revealed the card's reading, we both stared at each other and huge grins spread across both our faces. It was as if our entire conversation throughout the session had been scripted from this particular card reading, down to specific words and phrases.

If she was looking for confirmation that she was on the right track, she had found it. You can find this guidance and support to ground you on your present path too.

On the flip side, I've seen clients in my clinic who feel a little lost, yet they're very closed off to receiving guidance. They are stuck in their heads too much, focusing too much on the 'what' of our session, instead of the energy of it. They focus on what I'm doing and try to unpack what's happening in the session, instead of just flowing with whatever comes up.

When we fight, we don't flow. And when we don't flow, we stay stuck. If you feel stuck and lacking direction, and if you crave purpose, connection and feeling linked up to your true potential, you can look for signs all around you. Angel numbers, feathers fluttering in through windows, articles that keep popping up for you to read, people who come into your life at the perfect moment.

If it's confirmation you crave, just kindly ask the universe to show it to you. You don't need to be specific with which signs you're looking for, simply ask for some kind of confirmation or sign. It could be certain numbers that you continue to come across (there are lots of apps and books on angel numbers and their meanings) or feathers, coins or anything else.

Then let the signs come to you when you're ready to receive them. Don't let yourself get stuck in your head, constantly overthinking. Instead, let your heart do the thinking and creating. Heart thinking (or could we call it 'heartking'?) allows you to keep your fear out of the picture. The picture might still be a puzzle that isn't finished yet (some puzzles take t-i-m-e) but ... your level of 'heartking' is directly correlated to the depths of your connection to universal confirmation that says, *Sweet pea, you're on the right track.*

This track (your track) was made for you. Get. On. It. Believe it's yours and make it so.

Part Four

cleansing, balancing +
aligning your energies

Chapter 20

are you fuelling up or just filling up?

❧

It's so important that we know we can choose to fuel ourselves into action, create new opportunities to empower ourselves with compassion where none existed before, and illuminate ways to release some darkness and 'stuckness', where it's truly no longer appreciated or needed.

When I was constantly comparing myself to others, I'd often find myself mindlessly filling my time, by keeping my mind and emotions blocked to everything and anything I could have been doing to embrace true self-acceptance and self-empowerment.

You could take this chapter lightly and just look at the surface of your life ... where are you investing energy in your day-to-day life? Email? Social media? Stuck in the throes of self-comparison? Or you could choose to dive a little deeper in this chapter and uncover ways to release that feeling of simply filling yourself to exist, rather than fuelling yourself to thrive.

What are you doing with your hours?

It's time to decide whether you want to keep pushing yourself until you're blue in the face and exhausted, or whether you'd like to spend your time in a way that's more aligned with who you are, allowing you to create a life you love.

When we're stuck comparing ourselves to others, we often waste so much time in worry and negative thought patterns. We waste our time filling up with rubbish, instead of fuelling ourselves with positive things. We burn ourselves out trying to become the best version of ourselves, when there's a much easier, joyful and ease-filled way to live.

You'll always have to make choices about how you spend your time. Even as I write this book, I'm called to make decisions on how and when I spend my energy. I have slightly reduced my client sessions each week, so I have an extra day to write. I plan my time to allow myself space to write at the time of day I write best (mornings) and I'm not taking on any extra writing projects or interviews. Every thousand words I write for an article or interview is a thousand words I can't write for my book.

I have changed my email auto-responder to let people know I'm writing a book so I may be a little delayed in responding personally to them. Doing this has allowed me to create a little space in my life, in my calendar and in my energy. Yes, we all have the same amount of hours in a day as Einstein, Oprah and Beyoncé; it's what we do with them that counts.

When you feel called to say 'no' to something, think about what that allows you to say 'yes' to

I know that saying 'no' can seem impossible sometimes. But you know what feels even harder? Saying 'yes', then feeling squashed for time, resentful, exhausted and annoyed when it comes down to fulfilling your commitment. Not only are you allowed to say 'no', it's crucial that you discern when to do it. There are ways you can say 'no' with love. This helps to strengthen, protect and affirm your own boundaries, which actually helps strengthen your relationships.

Several months ago, I received a very long email from someone asking me to collaborate on a project. I instantly got the vibe that it wasn't right for me. While this person sounded lovely over email, I knew I'd have to say 'no'. It wasn't just a gut feeling that I didn't want to be involved in this project, but also my intuition whispering: *You have enough going on right now. If you take this on too, you'll feel pushed for time, resentful and tired. Just say 'no'.*

I emailed a very kind response and a very gentle refusal. I received a reply that was full of thanks and gratitude. My 'no' had been said in such a lovely way that I'd been profusely thanked for it! Good times.

Here are some tips to help you say no (so nicely)

'Should' is a warning word

There's a difference between giving **of** yourself and giving **up** yourself. There's a difference between doing something out of love and generosity, or doing something because you think you **should**, out of guilt or obligation. Anytime I add 'should' to a sentence, I know it's something I don't really want to be doing:

> *I should go see that person means I don't really want to, but I feel obligated.*

> *I should finish that blog post means I'm not actually that interested in writing about that topic, but I feel I need to finish it out of duty.*

And on it goes. Notice where and when you use the word 'should' in your inner dialogue. Catch yourself, and then ask yourself how you're really feeling. Do you really need to do the things you think you should be doing? If you truly wanted to do them, the word 'should' wouldn't enter your vocabulary at all.

Always thank the other person

If you can't take something on for a million reasons, don't feel the need to explain yourself. 'No' is a complete sentence (when said nicely and sometimes with other sentences around it).

Always offer an alternative

Do you have a resource, blog post, friend, colleague or another option you can direct someone to? If you can't help, maybe you know someone who can.

Be very kind but firm

It's okay to be honest but you don't need to over-explain. Saying things like 'I already have too much on my plate' or 'I can't create space for this right now' or 'I need to leave that afternoon open for myself' are all perfectly acceptable.

Back yourself

You wouldn't make a date with a friend or a dentist appointment and flake out at the last minute, would you? (Or maybe if it's the dentist, you might!) Make sure that if you're going to make a plan with yourself (to rest, take time off, slow down etc.), you back yourself and don't flake out on yourself. If you say you need to rest, then you need to rest … so rest.

Catch yourself before you fill yourself

You know those times when you're sitting on the couch just scrolling through your phone, and even while you're doing it, you know it's emptying you of some of your life–force? Yet you keep searching and scrolling, in case you find something that fills you up.

Maybe you're searching for something on Instagram or Facebook, or just mindlessly looking through your phone, your calendar, or your notes, in case something pops out that says: *Hey, you're worthy, I love you, you're doing an amazing job*. That might sound a bit strange, but even as I type this, I know I'm guilty of it too.

Perhaps you do what I used to do all the time; spend hours scrolling through other people's social media feeds, feeling smaller, less worthy and completely disempowered the longer you stay online? You fill up on mindless, endless, negative chit–chat, which leaves you with all-too-familiar feelings of not being good enough.

When I was stuck in the depths of comparison, I did this often. I knew that one way to get out was to create something that matched the vibration and beauty of whatever I was in awe of. Yet filling up on other peoples' work was blocking me from doing this.

Next time you catch yourself filling up in a way that doesn't benefit you (and you'll know what does and doesn't benefit you) back away from it. You don't have time for that anymore.

Do you purposefully overfill your cup?

Are you using busyness as life blinkers? Do you purposefully stuff the cracks of your life to the brim, so you can't see what you really need to be looking at? That's what obsessing over other peoples' work was doing for me. It was a way to fill up my day and my time, to fill up my life, even though every part of me knew I should get out of that trap. Sometimes I see this in my clients too, this kind of ignoring what's really going on for them under the surface.

When I'm feeling a bit drained and exhausted, or when I know I've been pushing myself too far or too hard, I'm still reminded to come back to what I know will really fuel me and not just fill me up with mindless nothingness and endless emptiness.

So many of us fill ourselves up with mindless busyness to pass the time and to feel falsely full and whole, as a way to keep our spiritual blinkers on. When we're busy, perhaps we're not thinking about the stuff we really need to be thinking about?

When we're immersed in things we never needed to step into, we can't take the necessary time to look after ourselves, to ask the tough questions and to create the space in which to answer them.

Sometimes all this talk of pushing ourselves to the limit can leave us a little exhausted. It's what we do at this point that determines whether we burn ourselves out or refuel and restore our energy.

Sometimes we fill up our time to procrastinate from working on ourselves or areas of our lives. It's resistance in every sense of the word. Is your 'filling up' and busyness a form of self-sabotage, or is there a secondary gain—a hidden benefit—in staying where you are and not replenishing yourself? Is there something that feels scary to deal with, something you don't want to face?

The best thing to do after asking yourself those questions is to reframe how you're fuelling yourself, so you can prevent burnout and fatigue, and stay committed to your path and purpose in the best possible way.

The 4 steps to reframing your refills

Step 1: Refine and define

Get really clear on how, where, why and when you're spending your energy. It could be on something big, such as your job, or a mindset or thought pattern that keeps coming up again and again. Is this refill truly fuelling and meeting a need you have, or are you wasting time and energy on it? Define your fuel. When you define what's been fuelling you, you'll be able to work out if it's raising your vibration or lowering it. If it's the latter, then you can take steps to remedy this.

Step 2: Reflect

Take some time to think about how this filling up is affecting you. Is it draining or expanding your energy levels? Is it changing your personality, lessening your patience or crushing your confidence?

Step 3: Release it

Give yourself express permission to release it. Acknowledge any guilt, shame or pain it was causing, surrender it up and say goodbye to it.

Step 4: *Replace it*

What can this be replaced with? How can you replenish yourself in a much more reliable and complete way? Could you delete a social media app from your phone and add a meditation app in its place? Can you pick up an old passion project or go back to an art class, instead of getting stuck in actionless fear every Sunday afternoon? How can you replace filling with fuelling? When can you start?

⟨⟩ Redirect to realign ⟨⟩

Is how you spend your time truly aligned with where you want to go in your life? Is there something you need to clear away in your life, in order to make this easier for you?

Perhaps in the beginning, noticing where and how you're spending your energy and investing your time then switching it up to start embracing more positive thoughts, activities and actions may feel challenging. But ultimately, it'll allow you to truly move through old stuff and create something new, to help you complete an old chapter, integrate your lessons learnt and manifest something exquisite into your life. Like so many things in life, it's your call. What will you choose?

⟨⟩ Who are you doing it for? ⟨⟩

Are you filling up your time to appear more successful, happier and more worthy in others' eyes? How can you recognise this, then remedy it? When I was stuck deep in my own comparison trap, I pushed myself to breaking point because I thought this would make me more worthy and more visible, not just on a personal level, but also in the eyes of the people to whom I was comparing myself.

You may have heard that introverts are perceived to be quiet, shy people, while extroverts are the opposite, loud and boisterous. But this isn't necessarily true. Introverts are people who enjoy recharging their energy on their own, but they may well be as happy up on stage in front of hundreds of people as they are on the couch on a rainy Sunday afternoon with a cup of hot tea (oh, that sounds kind of nice, right?).

This makes so much sense to me. I've never felt comfortable calling myself either an introvert or an extrovert, because I never felt I could completely relate to either of them. Now I know for sure I'm an introvert. If I have two or three arrangements or plans in a day, and they're with more than one or two people, I find it hard to move from one to the other without at least stopping off home for a breather.

Part of this is understanding and honouring your energetic boundaries too. That might sound ridiculous to someone who can easily hop from one social gathering to the next, but I need to ground myself and recharge before I spend a lot of time in a large group of people. And depending on the gathering, sometimes I leave feeling great and sometimes I leave feeling exhausted.

› What's your fuel? ‹

Now let's talk about how to best refuel yourself, then take action to do so. Are the activities you're pursuing or giving yourself permission to indulge in truly benefiting you, or to some extent, do you enjoy just filling the time, but not really fuelling up?

I know for me, having a secret (or just a quiet) place I can call my own is important for me to feel at peace and be able to fully let go and relax. Whether this means spending time alone or creating a space in my home, I honour this. Sometimes it just means I don't make any plans on a Sunday afternoon and spend it lying on my bed with books, notebooks, tea and maybe even a movie. I have no qualms about saying to friends, 'I need to keep part of the weekend free to do nothing; can we go for tea on Saturday afternoon instead of Sunday?'

The thought of this used to make me feel queasy, so much so that I'd fill my weekends with arrangement after arrangement leaving absolutely no time for myself. Even as I'd go from plan to plan (which kind of sounds like I was going from meeting to meeting, even though this was meant to be pleasure, not business) I'd find myself clenching my jaw or feeling breathless, a bit panicked and suffocated. I knew I was feeling resentful of my situation, which in the scheme of life is a wonderful situation. Of course, once I saw my friends, I was happy to be with them. But it didn't take away from the fact that I truly needed to create more space in my life to refuel myself in a way that felt good to me.

I want you to think back over the last week and think about how you've spent your energy, and whether it feels aligned to you. Another way to do this is to start right now and use a fresh week to keep a keen eye on how you spend your time. While sometimes it may seem indulgent to put yourself so high up on your priority list, it's essential. The more you practice caring for yourself, the more you'll be able to give back to the world and those around you.

You choose

Where's your energy being directed? Because if you don't like where you're directing it, you can change the direction. You can steer your own ship. And really, you're the only one who knows where you truly want to go and invest your time and energy anyway.

We have so many opportunities in every moment and in every day to choose how we fuel ourselves on a physical, mental, emotional and spiritual level, and how we change the course of our life; whether it's through upgrading our thoughts, attitudes, beliefs and mindsets, changing the way we do things, where we invest energy and how we choose to receive and absorb it back again, to the more tangible things such as what we eat and drink.

The message in this chapter is simple: you get to choose how to refuel yourself. And you get to give yourself permission to indulge in the self-care that will allow you to feel more confident, content and clear, as you make your way through your days without feeling like the only way forward is to compare yourself to everyone around you.

And the good news? Your permission slip to refuel and not just fill up can start at any time, and last forever. Every day you have a choice about whether you **fuel** yourself, or just **fill** yourself. Every day you can choose clarity, compassion and kindness, or heaviness, comparison and external validation.

It's important you give yourself permission to fuel, nourish and restore yourself, as a way to allow full integration of everything you're absorbing, receiving and nurturing in your life. It's when we pay ourselves a little more attention on the inner plane that our outer world can really flourish and feel more aligned with who we are, and how we want to show up in the world.

You have it in you to choose to empower yourself, by knowing how to fuel and support yourself on a mental and emotional level. You'll soon realise you can feel so much more connected to and supported by not only yourself, but the universe too.

But what happens when we don't give ourselves permission to rest, integrate, renew and restore? What happens when we keep pushing ourselves and fail to acknowledge our progress, never feeling aligned to transformation on a feminine, yin and nurturing level?

Well, we burn out, that's what happens. So let's look into this a little more deeply, because honestly the world doesn't need the burnt out, exhausted version of you.

Chapter 21

healing and balancing your four bodies

❧

I know I'm tired when three things happen:

1. I constantly tell my husband I'm tired and he tells me he knows because I just told him like two seconds ago;

2. I feel resentful with anything in my schedule that isn't relaxing on the couch or watching last night's episode of *Homeland*; and

3. I feel so teary and emotional that it's like I'm getting my period a thousand times over (even though I don't usually feel that emotional before my period).

My sister calls it being 'floppy' ... those days where you have very little energy to do anything more than flop onto your bed or the couch.

We could call it a side effect of busyness, this burnout and fatigue. And for the purpose of this chapter, we will.

When we fill every crack of our life with stuff, never resting, recovering or being truly present, we are stuck in busyness. This busyness affects us on many levels, through our four bodies; physical, mental, emotional and spiritual.

When our friends ask us how we're going and we tell them: 'We're busy, busy. Just. So. Busy!' then we could be on the verge of burning out. Sometimes this seems like a pretty cool place to be, because we fool ourselves into thinking we're being super productive, and very important, and we place huge importance on tiny, tiny tasks. But the reality is very different. It's tiring, exhaustive and draining.

When we could cry at the drop of a hat, when we can't wake up in the mornings, or make it through to 4pm without chocolate, or fall asleep at night, and when we feel sad, overwhelmed, emotional and disconnected to not just who we are but what we want, we're in the throes of fatigue. Sometimes, my clients who don't fully understand what fatigue and burnout are all about think they're lazy. But I have a message for you: you're not lazy ... you're tired.

There's a huge difference between fatigue and laziness, and I'm 99% sure you're not lazy. And guess what? If you are feeling lazy, you're probably just exhausted and need some deep rest time anyway.

If you're a striving, perfectionist comparer, I could almost bet you're on a sliding scale somewhere between adrenal depletion and incredible vitality ... yet everyday you edge closer to the burnout end of the graph. And I could also bet (and I'm not even a betting woman) that this is causing you to feel exasperated in some aspect of your life. Perhaps you feel like you're running in circles and getting nowhere, that you're not good enough to be better so you'll just stay where you are, because you feel that no matter how hard you try, it's just not going happen for you anyway.

ℰ Give yourself deep rest time ℐ

Energetically, when you feel tired, you hold onto more trapped emotions. Your body tries to disengage you from the emotional pain and physical issues you may be experiencing through pushing yourself too hard, so those emotions get energetically stuck in you. They may be stuck in your meridians (energy channels that flow up and down your body), your chakra system, muscles, joints, tissues or somewhere else on your energetic or physical plane.

So your busyness isn't just affecting your ability to schedule in an extra lunch date or a long weekend; your busyness is affecting your energy on every level of your body, your self-confidence, self-worth and self-acceptance. And it's time to remedy this.

I know how easy it is to push yourself right through to fatigue, then way past it, and still feel as though you haven't done enough. Rest isn't something we need to earn. Unfortunately, it's during those times we tell ourselves all the things we must be doing, instead of telling ourselves we need to rest and do nothing else.

As I write this, I've actually given myself an entire day off and it was blissful. After a breakfast of poached eggs on spelt sourdough with avocado, and grabbing a takeaway latte, I hopped back into bed, bought a new book on my iPad and lay there for hours. I had a lazy lunch with my family, then back to my book I went. I picked up my laptop once, when an idea I wanted to add to my book dropped into my head, but then I went back to resting. A couple of hours later, after giving myself express permission to do nothing, another little spark of inspiration made itself known, so I find myself at my laptop again. But there was no stress or expectation around this. There was no guilt for taking time off, away from work or friends or appointments.

You need this time in your life too; whether you're a parent, friend, business owner, colleague, sibling or something else … you need this time. In fact, if you are the busy type, you need more of this time, even more than you think.

We'll spend a little time now unpacking what it means when we keep pushing ourselves, and look at how to re-energise ourselves, balance and align our energies, and release any and all guilt associated with self-care and slowing down. At the risk of sounding like a lame cliché, slowing down is the new black, and if we're to do well and feel well in our lives, it's important to embrace this. And only **you** can make this so.

✃ Are you driving yourself to exhaustion? ✄

When we drive ourselves to the edges of our perfectionism to prove our self-worth and seek external validation, we may also drive ourselves to exhaustion. I've done it, many times in the past, and if you're reading this right now it's likely you know exactly what I'm talking about.

We can't keep pushing ourselves to exhaustion because it keeps us from hearing our higher self's guidance, from listening to the voice that wants us to know we're so worthy, and good enough as we are.

Often, when our bodies are feeling stressed and strained, our emotions will feel very intense too. In *Metaphysical Anatomy*, when talking about emotions for depleted adrenals Evette Rose says:

> *You worry too much about life … Creating unrealistic scenarios in your mind and then acting emotionally as if it has already happened is draining … You have little energy to give and share with others, so you have begun to withdraw from your environment. This is your way of setting boundaries and conserving energy.*

On the flip side, before you hit the exhaustion stage your body is probably in overdrive, trying to create extra energy for all you're expending. When we're in this state, Rose says we often feel as though we're all over the place; we unconsciously create circumstances where we feel trapped and this leads to more stress and resentment. In this state, we're constantly being triggered in the fight or flight stress response mode, we're constantly feeling emotionally chaotic and wishy-washy, under pressure yet lacking structure, support and direction.

To heal from this and release these trapped emotions and old patterning, it's important to understand that we don't just live in our physical body; we also embody a mental, emotional and spiritual side and energy. To live a life of self-worth, acceptance and confidence, it's crucial to look after all four of your bodies.

Are you listening to what your body is saying?

It's time to look at the signs of burnout and how to start healing and balancing your four bodies; how to understand what your four bodies are trying to tell you when you're on the verge of burning out (or when you're already there), and how to remedy this to keep them healthy, balanced and aligned.

A little while ago I went away for the weekend with a bunch of people, some of whom I knew, and many I didn't. While the weekend had many lovely, fun moments, it was also crowded with activities I don't enjoy, foods I rarely eat and personalities that I didn't completely vibe with.

My throat felt a little sore on the Sunday, and by the time I woke up on the Monday after I could barely swallow. I didn't have the flu, or a headache or a fever. I just had the most intensely painful throat I can remember. It was so sore, and it didn't let up, so I went to see my family doctor (he's an integrative doctor and also a homoeopath). He took one look at my throat and told me I had an incredibly large ulcer at the back of my throat.

I knew why; it wasn't just because I'd spent three nights in air-conditioning that I couldn't adjust, or going from hot to cold temperatures. It was because the entire weekend had been filled with things that didn't sit well with me, yet I couldn't use my voice to speak up and change anything, because everything had been pre-organised.

Our bodies are sensitive, intelligent and protective. On some level, my body wanted to protect me from the strong emotions I was feeling when I felt the situation was out of control and I was completely out of my comfort zone. Usually, I find it very easy to speak my truth, and I'm not afraid of speaking up. Except on this weekend I couldn't, for many reasons. So the energy of the emotions and the truth that I couldn't express had to be funnelled somewhere. My throat—and that massive, painful ulcer—gave me the message I needed.

You may be feeling all sorts of niggles, pains and illnesses. If so, I can tell you that much of what you're feeling physically is because of what's going on for you on a mental, emotional and spiritual level.

Anything you're feeling physically may have an emotional root, and often does. When I was stuck learning lesson after lesson about how to release myself from comparison and create healthier boundaries, I was getting those heart palpitations I mentioned earlier. Yet there was nothing physically wrong with my heart; my doctor and a cardiologist told me this. On some level, I knew it too.

Energetically, our hearts hold the vibration of not just love for others, but also love, forgiveness and compassion for ourselves. I had no compassion or love for myself when I was comparing myself to others, hence my constant heart palpitations. I was pushing myself to my limit every single day, with zero forgiveness or love for where I was or who I was.

⟪⟫ What are the signs of burnout? ⟪⟫

When you've been pushing yourself for too long, your body will let you know about it, whether it's on a physical, mental, emotional or spiritual level. In this chapter, we'll dive deep into what you can do to heal from adrenal depletion on every level.

Our adrenal glands, small walnut-sized glands that sit atop our kidneys, are important glands that help to regulate our body's energy and protect us from stress. No matter what kind of stress we're going through, be it mental, emotional, physical, environmental or otherwise, our adrenals will take a hit.

And stress is accumulative. So if you work in a stressful job, travel a lot, eat unhealthy food, frequently fight with your partner and have a bad cold that has lingered for weeks, that's stress after stress after stress that your poor adrenal glands are trying to protect you from.

The list of symptoms of adrenal fatigue and burnout extends much further than just fatigue, exhaustion, brain fog and decreased productivity. As James L. Wilson says in *Adrenal Fatigue*, it includes other physical, mental and emotional symptoms such as insomnia, difficulty waking up in the morning, stress, anxiety, panic attacks, depression, teariness, restlessness, achy and painful joints and legs, difficulty falling asleep and waking up, digestive issues, cravings for sugar, salt, fat and carbs, dizziness on standing, heart palpitations, lowered immunity, less enjoyment in life, low libido, low tolerance and easily irritated, overwhelm and osteoporosis.

✁ Healing foods ✁

There are so many beautiful healing foods you can include in your day to improve adrenal function and support your energy levels. To begin, look at your overall diet and ensure there's adequate protein (such as grass-fed animal protein, eggs, organic/grass-fed dairy, nuts, seeds, poultry, fish and seafood); good fats (avocado, nuts, seed and their cold-pressed oils, including olive oil, organic butter and coconut oil); fruits and vegetables (including lots of leafy greens and brightly-coloured vegetables); healthy carbohydrates (such as sourdough bread, oats, brown rice, quinoa, millet, root veggies and even a little white potato with the skin on, which is super high in Vitamin C, needed for proper adrenal function). Fluids are also important.

One thing I always suggest to clients with fatigue is Himalayan salt. While many people may consume too much salt, they're most likely consuming too much of the processed, refined white stuff, not the natural mineral-rich Himalayan variety. It might sound surprising, but salting your food and water (yes, your water) is incredibly beneficial for adrenal fatigue, says Wilson in *Adrenal Fatigue*.

This is because it helps to balance sodium levels in our bodies which can often be low when fatigued. This is caused by a lack of the hormone aldosterone (which controls fluid in the body). If you feel that you drink a lot of water and never absorb it, if you get dizzy on standing, if you often feel very thirsty, then add some Himalayan salt to your food plus a pinch or two in the morning and at around 2–3pm. This will be so supportive for you.

ᴄᴐ Foods to eat less of ᴐ

It's important you reduce or avoid all the usual less-than-healthy suspects such as refined, white and processed sugar, alcohol, too much caffeine and high intakes of refined and processed foods.

I don't subscribe to the idea that we must never eat sugar again; I believe there is beauty and nourishment in fruits, honey and the natural sugars found in our food.

Of course, everything in moderation … including moderation. A couple of pieces of dark chocolate and a glass of red wine can do you as much good as an apple with almond butter, if you're enjoying it in the right mindset. So please don't be harsh on yourself; moderation is queen, but kindness is king.

It's also important to ensure you keep your blood sugar levels stable, as there's a strong link between adrenal function, energy and healthy blood sugar levels. Aim to eat breakfast in the first hour after rising. To avoid low blood sugar levels (hypoglycaemia), eat every three to four hours and ensure you include protein and good fats in your meals and snacks. You may also enjoy eating meals that combine protein, fats and carbohydrates, because this helps your body receive energy from food at different rates which will support your energy levels. Carbohydrates release energy first, then proteins, while fat takes longer, so you'll receive a slow-release of energy between meals.

᥉ Supplements to take ᧒

I know some people shy away from supplements for all manner of reasons, and that's so fine if it's your preference. I usually treat my clients with a combination of kinesiology, energetic essences, foods and herbal medicines, but there are times when some good basic supplements can do absolute wonders for a depleted, tired body.

In all honesty, it's not that I don't believe we can get everything we need from food; it's just that when we're in a very depleted state, high-quality supplements at a therapeutic dose can speed up recovery and help our bodies function optimally, faster.

Here are some nutrients I recommend to clients feeling fatigued:

Vitamin D

This important vitamin not only helps support our immune system (which can become run down in adrenal fatigue), it's also been found to protect against cancer and depression.

Vitamin B Complex

This is called a complex because it's all the B vitamins (B1, B2, B3, B5, B6, B7 (biotin), B9 (folic acid), B12) together. The B vitamins are a crucial factor in the energy cycle (known as the Krebs cycle) as well as mood, energy, hormone balance, digestion and metabolism of food, and so much more.

Fish oils

Very good quality fish oils will reduce inflammation, which will improve your wellbeing and mood, and even help to balance hormones.

Vitamin C

Vitamin C is very concentrated in the adrenal glands, so when we're tired we must replenish it. It's very important in a healthy immune system too, as well as being a potent antioxidant to protect against the damaging effects of stress.

Magnesium

This calming mineral will soothe stressed, anxious nerves, relax muscles and help you sleep. It also increases energy and can help with low moods.

CoQ10

Think of this nutrient as an oxygenator of all your cells. Whichever cell needs oxygen in your body (um, all of them!) will benefit from CoQ10, especially your heart. It may also reduce migraine headaches and restless legs. In fact, people who take statins (for high cholesterol) should really be on CoQ10 too (as well as St Mary's Thistle for liver support), as statins block the production of CoQ10, sometimes resulting in restless legs and muscle pain.

Healing herbs

Using herbal medicines is one of my favourite ways to heal the body and bring about balance. The following herbs are beautiful for soothing, healing, toning, calming and energising the body as a whole.

Bacopa

This beautiful herb works to calm anxiety while also improving mental cognition, making it wonderful for work-related stress, where you need to feel calm but totally in the zone.

Chamomile

You've probably heard of this herb and perhaps drink it as a tea. It's calming for the nervous system and wonderful for Irritable Bowel Syndrome or any digestive issues resulting from (or causing!) emotional and mental distress.

Ginsengs

There are three main ginsengs I use in my clinic: American, Korean and Siberian. They work in slightly different ways. American ginseng is beautiful to use when you're feeling very low and depleted, as it's not very stimulating but very healing. Siberian ginseng works to increase your body's ability to adapt to a range of stressors, while also increasing mood and boosting your immunity. Korean ginseng is brilliant for fatigue. It's like a spark plug for your cells, although it can be a little too stimulating for some people, e.g. if they're too drained and exhausted or sensitive to caffeine, even though there's no caffeine in the herb.

Kava

One of the best herbs for anxiety, this herb has been found to be as effective as benzodiazepines without the side effects (and yes, if you've ever been to Fiji, this is the same kava you'd have drunk in a kava ceremony). It also increases cognition, without leaving you feeling drowsy, making it the perfect pre-exam/interview/presentation herb too. Before I spoke at my first live event, I downed a lot of kava!

Lavender

Blissfully calming, taking this herb will help you have a restful sleep and will improve your mood. As a plus, it's also great for candida and fungal infections.

Lemon balm

Another soothing, calming nervine tonic herb (meaning it's balancing for the nervous system), this herb works wonders for insomnia, anxiety and stress impacting your digestive system.

Licorice and Rehmannia

These herbs have been used in combination for centuries as adrenal tonics. Separately, they work in different ways; together they're wonderful for fatigue. Licorice is anti-inflammatory, great to take if you get dizzy on standing, and is also used for sugar cravings (linked to adrenal depletion) and for coughs. Rehmannia is also incredibly anti-inflammatory and is used to curb sugar cravings and to cool an overheated body.

Passionflower

This calming herb will reduce anxiety, stress and restlessness and improve sleep. It's wonderful where there are heart palpitations or you feel 'wired but tired'.

Rhodiola

If I had a favourite herb (which I don't, because just look at how amazing this small handful of herbs all are!) it would be rhodiola. There's a concept in natural medicine called *The Doctrine of Signatures*, which states that the way a plant, fruit or vegetable looks can give a hint to its use in the body. Think of a walnut; it kind of looks like a brain, and is great for brain health. A tomato has four chambers like the heart and contains the antioxidant lycopene, which is great for heart health.

So back to rhodiola … it's an arctic herb and grows in the most difficult conditions in Europe and North America. It's been used as a tonic herb for centuries. It thrives in icy, wet, freezing conditions. It thrives, no matter where it lives, or what's going on around it. And that's why it's one of my favourite herbs. Rhodiola improves our mood, mental and physical endurance, cognition, memory and learning. It's been found to be anti-tumour and incredibly high in antioxidants. It also improves ovulation. It's like the Superman of herbs. Totally not my favourite though. I couldn't do that to the other herbs.

St John's Wort

This herb is well known for its mood-boosting abilities. It's been found to be **as effective as antidepressants**, without the side effects. It also helps to reduce stress and I've found, through my clients, it helps to improve emotional resilience. As a great plus, it's anti-viral and specific for cases of glandular fever, which can cause fatigue. It's a winner, and will find its way into most of my clients' herbal formulas at some stage of us working together.

Don't take this herb if you're on oral contraceptives, antidepressants or other medications, as it speeds up the metabolism of certain medications through the liver, making them less effective. (It can be taken with some medications, but best to check with a naturopath or herbalist.)

Withania

Another of my favourites, this Ayuverdic herb is great for fatigue and lethargy. It is also useful if you've been unwell for long periods of time. It calms anxiety, is blood building and nourishing (making it great for anaemia and vegetarians or vegans). It also works as an adaptogen, helping your body adapt to all kinds of stressors.

℃ How to take herbs ℘

Herbs are usually taken as liquids or tablets. Dosages will vary depending on what's going on for you, and your constitution. Sometimes you'll find them in powder formulations, especially if you're seeing a Chinese medicine practitioner or an acupuncturist who prescribes herbs.

You can also drink them as teas, however they won't be as therapeutic or as active as a liquid herb. That's because in liquid formulas the herb is usually extracted with ethanol, which is an alcohol (it's metabolised by the liver very quickly), which allows the most therapeutic action. The amount of ethanol used depends on which part of the herb is used, e.g. a bark may need more ethanol to extract the active constituents than a flower or berry.

Herbs are best taken under the advice of someone you trust and who's been trained in herbal medicine, such as a qualified herbalist or naturopath (not a nutritionist—they aren't trained in herbs).

Healing breathing

This isn't the kind of book that'll tell you: *Digestion begins with chewing in the mouth* (because I feel like you know that already); nor is it the kind of book that'll tell you: *Breathing is so important for our life* (because again, I'm pretty sure you know that).

However this **is** the kind of book that'll gently remind you how important it is to make space for deep, clear, even breathing. Making this space will allow you to release some stress; allow new insights to drop in; allow you to make realisations for new ways you'd like to press forward in life; and allow you to breathe out guilt, grief and regret.

Energetically, the lung meridian relates to feelings of going with the flow and breathing easily in life, our energy, and of feeling light and carefree. On the flip side, imbalances or blockages and over or under energies can relate to feelings of grief, guilt and regret.

My lungs have always been one of the first organs of my body to let me know when something is up. So I know firsthand how crucial it is to care for our lungs, not only physically but also on an energetic and emotional level.

Here are a few ways to make space for breath and keep your lungs energetically clean and clear:

Give yourself time each day to simply breathe

You can call it a meditation if you wish, or you could just sit down on the couch and take some calming, deep breaths. Let your mind wander wherever it wants to, and bring it back to your breath whenever you feel the need to. Exhale.

Use essential oils

You can burn certain essential oils to help invigorate your breathing and also calm your mind and body down. My favourites include rosemary, grapefruit, ylang ylang and lavender.

Work with your guilt, grief, or regret, then let it go

Sometimes we can push ourselves so hard that we create excess struggle where none needs to exist. This can result in feelings of grief and regret, which can get stuck in our lungs, exacerbating any previous lung weakness, e.g. asthma or contributing to lung conditions, e.g. bronchitis or chest infections.

This has happened to me, resulting in bronchitis and then acute asthma that knocked me sideways and kept me up at night, always between 1am and 3am, when our livers are energetically more active. This was an indication to me that I was finding it hard to process, detoxify and let go of my guilt or grief, ergo more coughing at 2am (liver time). You can see how this all relates quite specifically to how we're feeling, what we're thinking, and what we're going through in our lives.

It took months of work (kinesiology, energetic essences, yoga, journaling, automatic writing, stillness, self-permission to release and let go plus lots of deep sighing) to help me release what needed to be released.

How often do you catch yourself holding your breath when stressed?

When I was a make-up artist (before my career switch to natural and energetic medicine), I would hold my breath without thinking whenever I did black liquid eyeliner on a model. This is obviously not life-changing, but it's a simple example of how, when we're stressed, we don't breathe properly. When we feel stressed, tired and anxious we don't breathe as deeply and this, in turn, affects our sympathetic nervous system (the fight or flight mechanism), keeping us in a stressed state.

I recently saw a client who constantly felt as though she couldn't breathe properly. Throughout the session, lung acupressure points came up, as did an energetic essence that has eucalyptus in it (which is great for chesty and congested coughs). It also came up that she was energetically holding on to a lot of grief, guilt and regret; our lungs hold these energies when they're in an imbalanced state. I didn't give her breathing exercises; I simply put on some soothing music and left the room while I made her liquid herbs, and asked her to just lie down and let the session integrate. Simply by creating the space to do so, she started to breathe deeply and she commented that her chest felt so much lighter.

You can calm your body down by taking slow, deep breaths, or by doing a breathing exercise. My favourite breathing exercise, if I'm feeling a little on the jittery side, is alternative nostril breathing. Search YouTube for videos on this and find one that vibes with you. It's so simple to do, and I know it puts me in such a Zen state. It's beautiful.

Self-care and healing therapies

When I went through my first experience of burnout, I decided to really invest in self-care. I gave myself a weekly allowance for self-care, and revelled in the freedom to use that money, guilt free. Whether it was something as small as a manicure, a long lunch date by myself in a cafe, a massage or something else, it felt so luxurious and I felt so pampered. I kept this up for a couple of months until I started to feel more energised. I highly recommend this self-care strategy, sans guilt.

ꞔꞔ Exercise and movement ꝺꝺ

When you're feeling exhausted, going to the gym six times a week, running for an hour a day or doing heavy weights isn't the most beneficial thing to be doing to your body. Exercise is a form of stress, which can work for us or against us. It's working for us when we stress our muscles with weights or body weight, give them time to repair and then see our muscles grow and tone. However when we're run-down, pushing ourselves at the gym only adds more stress to an already stressed system. In fact, high intensity exercise actually depletes our immune system, leading to a greater chance of us getting sick.

I recommend gentle walks (preferably in or near nature, if possible), gentle yoga sessions (this can be hatha, yin and even vinyasa flow classes, but not Bikram) and other low-impact, low-intensity exercises like barre classes, Pilates or even spin.

If you've ever had body image issues, I know it can feel detrimental to reduce your exercise in intensity or frequency, but this really is for your highest good. Your body needs a chance to replenish itself, repair and heal. By engaging in less strenuous exercise, you'll help lower your body's stress levels while still benefiting from exercise and movement. And when you're less stressed, weight loss and weight balance will actually be easier, both physiologically and psychologically.

Did you know that a yoga class actually clears and balances your chakras? When I discovered this, I found it fascinating. Yes, simply going to yoga and flowing, bending and breathing helps to shift stuck energy and rebalance our chakras and meridians. Magic.

I found more fascinating information about how exercise helps us clear and shift mental and emotional fog and stuckness in a brilliant book called *Spark*, by John J. Ratey. He explains how exercise is even more important for our brains than for our bodies, and pulls together the most incredible research to support this. Whether it's to treat depression, anxiety, stress or hormonal imbalances, daily exercise can change your brain in the most incredible ways.

Ratey says: *The great thing about exercise is that it fires up the recovery process in our muscles and our neurons. It leaves our bodies and minds stronger and more resilient, better able to handle future challenges, to think on our feet and adapt more easily.*

So that walk, yoga class or jog around the park you indulge in each morning is not just part of a healthy lifestyle and healthy body. It's one of the best things you can do for a healthy brain; a brain that allows you to focus, feel happy, sleep deeply, protect yourself, reduce stress and anxiety, learn and memorise things, balance hormones and so much more.

Meditation

I'm a big fan of meditation, in all its forms. I will often do a guided meditation, such as a chakra cleanse meditation to end off my day or clear my mind in the middle of the day. I recommend this to all my clients too.

Apart from what all the research says, giving your mind time to shut down is important. My best ideas will often come to me after a few minutes of stillness.

If meditating feels out of reach, try this …

Imagine your mind is like a computer with lots of browser windows open. Sit down, take a few settling breaths and imagine closing down each of these open browser windows, until they're all shut down. Then focus on the quiet and calm of your breathing for several moments, until you've decided it's time to reopen some of the browser windows. You don't need all of them anymore, so just pick a few. Once your refreshed browser is ready, you can open your eyes and carry on with your day.

❧ Rest ☙

There's no other way to say this; if you're tired, you need to rest. You need to clear your schedule, create space and give yourself permission to enjoy it, guilt free. And please be open to rest time coming up in times when you don't **think** you need it. A little while ago I had only one client booked in for my entire week. With hindsight, I can see it's time I truly needed (in fact, I started writing my book **that** week!). The week before, I'd told a friend I had to start creating more space for my writing, and then—bam—an entire week appeared for me.

When we ask for something, be it more time, space or whatever else we need (whether we know it or not), the universe will deliver it in some way. So be ready, with open, excited arms.

Releasing overwhelm, then feeling on top of things again

So often, when a client lies down on the kinesiology bed in my clinic and we start setting goals for their session, they'll say, 'I want to feel on top of things again.'

I understand what it's like when your schedule is so full and you feel you can barely get anything done now, so you wonder how you'll get **more** done when you're taking time out to care for yourself. But here's what I know: when you're approaching your life and your to-do list from a space of feeling full, whole, happy and grounded, you'll get so much done in much less time.

You'll start feeling more on top of things when **you** are on the top of your to-do list. I promise, this is true. The reason you're not feeling on top of things isn't because you're not doing enough; it's because you're exhausted, and feeling as if you can't cope. The sooner you start to care for yourself on a very deep level, the sooner you'll get more done in less time, and love your life even more for it.

Releasing guilt and caring for
yourself to the max

Releasing guilt and emotional baggage that's causing you to feel that you aren't worthy of self-care can be as simple as giving yourself permission to release it, or as difficult as continuing to make yourself feel guilty about it.

I remember when I realised I truly had to start looking after myself and not feel guilty about it. While it felt a little difficult in the beginning, it got easier and easier the more I let myself enjoy it.

Think about how you can start really releasing guilt and deeply looking after yourself, and then begin ... today.

Chapter 22

creating healthy energetic boundaries

Part of healing from fatigue, depletion of any kind, burnout and comparison is about creating healthy energetic boundaries and enforcing them with love. Energetic boundaries define our territory, from what we say 'yes' or 'no' to; to how we let others treat us and communicate with us; to whether we feel drained or protected when we stand in a busy room full of strong personalities.

Your boundaries are invisible to your eye, but powerful to your soul and spirit. When they're healthy, we feel protected, grounded and balanced. We're easily able to deflect energies and advances we don't need or feel aligned to, and we can protect our energy from people who otherwise would drain or deplete us.

However, if there are any 'chinks in the armour' so to speak, we may feel easily drained by others, overwhelmed by others' energies, taken for granted or taken advantage of, or lacking in resilience and inner strength. It's like wearing a zip-up sweater that's been unzipped, allowing in a chilly wind when you'd prefer to feel zipped up and warm.

When our boundaries aren't strong and healthy, we may make decisions that don't feel aligned with who we are; we may feel exhausted by spending time with certain people or simply by thinking about being around certain people. We find it difficult to speak up, we pick up and absorb other peoples' worries, fears or concerns, and we may even feel physically ill.

In *Energetic Boundaries*, Cyndi Dale says that when our boundaries are violated, three main things will happen:

1. **Our boundaries become rigid or immobilised**, making us feel as if we need to shut down to others, losing trust in them and feeling isolated and alienated.
2. **Our boundaries become permeable**, meaning we're easily swept aside, ignored, used, taken advantage of or left unrewarded.
3. **Our boundaries become full of holes**, meaning there are gaps in our energetic boundaries, like doors left open for other people's energies to enter, even diseases and negative mindsets or patterns. In this state, we lose our own life-force.

So you can see how crucial it is that we not only create our healthy boundaries but that we affirm and enforce them with love.

How to set boundaries

I usually set boundaries by simply setting them, and then doing something to enforce them. Whether that means setting an intention, writing something out in my journal, speaking up and telling someone how I'm feeling or simply removing myself from a situation I don't want to be in (or ensuring I don't find myself there in the first place), it works wonders for my energy, sense of grounding and confidence.

The first time I realised I really didn't have healthy, strong boundaries I was left reeling. There were three incidents in the same week where I was left feeling bitter, resentful, angry and emotionally charged. And all because I lacked clear boundaries, because I let other people's stuff become attached to me and because the flimsy boundaries I did have weren't being enforced properly.

Since then, I've made sure to keep my boundaries well protected (and loved) and ensured I kept my energy protected, balanced and 100% my own. I do this not just because I have compassion for myself, but also because I have compassion for others. When my boundaries are healthy, I'm able to extend much more love without burning myself out, letting others attach to my energy or hurting myself to help someone else.

❮❮ Healthy, firm boundaries ❯❯

If we leave ourselves open without healthy boundaries, we're more likely to surrogate others' energies. This may happen in the physical presence of others, over the phone, email, Skype or we may even pick them up just by scrolling mindlessly through social media.

Surrogating means we've taken on someone else's energy, either because we haven't protected our own boundaries enough or because we subconsciously feel we're helping someone else by taking on their 'stuff'.

You know when you go for lunch with a friend who's constantly telling you how awful and terrible everything is in her life, and so you leave the lunch date feeling drained or depressed? I've had people in my life who I allowed to make me feel drained even before I saw them. In these circumstances, I take steps to protect my energy, which I'll help you learn to do in the next few chapters.

(As a positive aside ... when I do kinesiology sessions with clients over Skype, I surrogate their energy, with their permission, in order to do their balance. But I always clear their energy from my field afterwards.)

Hiro Boga, a business strategist and energy alchemist, says: *Discerning between feelings and thoughts that are your own, and those that are the result of energy you've absorbed, begins with knowing yourself.* It's so important to realise when you may be surrogating for someone else, and then take steps to protect, cleanse and balance your energy.

Love your boundaries, and they'll love you back

When we are first called on in our lives to create boundaries, it feels scary. We wonder how to set them, how to enforce them, but mostly we worry that we'll upset or offend people. We feel guilty for saying 'no', for saying 'yes', for saying what we feel or asking for what we need. We put everyone above and before ourselves and we feel simultaneously guilty and resentful; all the while knowing we can't keep this up, knowing we could be doing things differently but feeling ashamed or unable to make the change.

The truth is very different to what we usually tell ourselves though. If you create boundaries from a place of love and self-care, not fear and panic, you'll actually be rewarded for it. Can you imagine? Making a mark in your energetic world and being rewarded for looking after yourself? It's an incredible feeling when you notice it, and you will notice it … but only when you start to create healthy boundaries and then lovingly enforce them, without the guilt.

Weird and wonderful

Your boundaries can even love you back in weird and unexpected ways. Sometimes you'll be tested on how much you want something, or how strong and firm your boundaries truly are.

I remember a time where I kept seeing clients who weren't ideally aligned to me or my work. They weren't bad people, it's just that I knew I probably wasn't the best practitioner for them, because my passions and interest lay elsewhere. I had a loving little chat with my journal and the universe:

Hey, I'm loving that my client calendar is busy but … I don't think I'm seeing the right clients for me and my business. Could we do something about this, please? I'm ready to see the clients I know I can help the most.

I wrote out a few lines describing the kinds of clients I really wanted to be attracting. To help myself feel more aligned to this, I did a little kinesiology balance on myself, using some tools and elements I'll take you through in the next section.

Over the next few days, three new clients booked in who were all completely unsuited to my business, to such a degree it was slightly laughable (in a nice way!). I felt like they hadn't even read my website or knew what I did. I rang each client up and explained that I felt they'd be better looked after by a colleague, and referred them on. They were so grateful for my honesty and gladly cancelled their session with me. Hence, I created more space for my ideal client.

While I was so happy with how things had worked out, I was also a little taken aback. Hadn't I just literally asked the universe to send me my **ideal** clients? Hadn't I set firm, healthy boundaries and aligned myself to them?

The answer hit me straightaway; the universe **had** heard my request and yes, I had set the right boundaries. Now I was being tested. How much did I want this? How truly aligned was I? I stuck to my initial boundary setting and just a few days later, new and wonderfully ideal clients booked in. So while I'm sure that was a test, I'm also pretty sure I passed with flying colours.

ᚳᚷ Protect, cleanse and balance your energy ᚷᚷ

You can easily strengthen and affirm your energetic boundaries with love, as well as protect, cleanse and balance your energy. Luckily, there are many ways for us to do this.

A few of my favourite ways include doing a grounding meditation, going for a walk along the beach taking deep, grounding breaths, having a kinesiology or reiki session, having an Epsom salts bath, setting intentions/affirmations which can be used in conjunction with kinesiology and energy balancing techniques (which I'll take you through soon), as well as essences, sprays and crystals (which we'll talk about in upcoming chapters).

ᚳᚷ Intentions and affirmations ᚷᚷ

Simply setting the intention that you want to protect your energy is powerful, sending a ripple effect throughout your energy systems.

Choose any of these intentions and affirmations and use them throughout your day:

≳ *I'm 100% aligned to protecting my own energy*
≳ *I easily protect my own energy*
≳ *My energy is 100% my own*
≳ *It's safe and easy for me to feel clear, protected and grounded in my energies*
≳ *I easily protect my boundaries with love*
≳ *I have clear, strong and healthy boundaries that keep me safe and grounded*
≳ *My energy is clear, balanced and grounded*
≳ *It's safe and easy for me to create boundaries and affirm them with love*

To reduce any stress on these intentions/affirmations, you may wish to use them while also doing the *Emotional Stress Release* technique that I'll teach you in Chapter 24.

❦ A clean slate ❧

When you truly let yourself take care of your four bodies, you open the doorway to soul-expanding discovery of self. You give yourself a chance to create a clean slate each day, to create from your heart and follow its lead and to not get tangled up with the ins and outs of your daily world. Comparison, overwhelm and struggle feel at their strongest when we're exhausted, drained and depleted.

When we're exhausted and not looking after ourselves, we leave cracks open where these negative emotions lie dormant, getting stuck in our tissues, our joints, our muscles and our minds, hearts and souls.

In the next chapter, we'll be looking at extra tools you can use to clear, align and balance your energies on a very deep level.

Part Five

your energetic toolkit

Chapter 23

clearing energetic blocks

*If you truly want to grow spiritually, you'll realize that
keeping your stuff is keeping you trapped.*

Michael A. Singer, *The Untethered Soul*

I'm not a handyman, but I have the most incredible toolkit
on the planet. There are no nails, hammers or saws
in this toolkit. But it can help you put things together,
connect, ground and release what needs to be connected,
grounded and let go. It can help you clear blockages and
anything else that is trapped or stuck. It's not expensive or
difficult to put together, and while it may need topping up
sometimes, it can grow, deepen and develop into something
that is truly magnetic, vibrational, pulsing.

It's made up of tools to help you raise your vibration, get
unstuck and live a truly and uniquely fulfilling life. It's an
energetic toolkit. I'll explain what you need to know about
each of the tools that'll help you let go of fear, resistance and

worry and embrace your intuition, guidance and personal power. I'll also offer up suggestions of tools you can add to your own toolkit, based on what I've personally used and loved.

These are the tools and resources that have helped me on my journey. They're what I lean towards when I feel a little blocked, stuck or misaligned. And they're the tools I provide for my clients and online course participants.

Falling into alignment with our true selves—the part of us that knows we're worthy, and who can feel confident and courageous in our actions and clear in our thoughts—becomes so much easier when we're able to energetically clear the blocks that are holding us back.

In the last few chapters we went over some ways to start clearing and healing your four bodies, with lots of physical and tangible tools you can use to support this. In the following chapters, we'll talk about other, lesser known—but incredibly healing and powerful—tools you can use to clear energetic blocks.

I want you to know that when you're feeling stuck, unsupported, wishy-washy or overwhelmed it doesn't need to last and stay stuck in you. Michael A. Singer, author of *The Untethered Soul*, speaks about how to view inner pain in what I think is quite a wonderful way. He says, *If you want to be free, simply view inner pain as a temporary shift in your energy flow.* If pain is a temporary shift in our energy flow, then surely we can open up to shifting its flow back into alignment with ourselves? I believe so and, lucky us, we live in a world where there are so many incredible tools, therapies and modalities we can embrace and employ, to help us shift out of this pain and into flow, alignment, ease, peace and grace.

In this section we'll look at how to clear and balance the energy system through spiritual and kinesiology tools. As I mentioned, I'll also offer up some ideas on how you can create your own energetic toolkit too. Each tool has its own mini chapter, so it's super easy for you to dive in again and again. Let's get started.

Chapter 24

emotional stress release

ⱺⱷⱺ

Emotional Stress Release (ESR) is a simple kinesiology technique that I use in my clinic on an almost daily basis. Not to be confused with the Emotional Freedom Technique (usually just called EFT), this powerful and gentle healing technique is one of the first kinesiology techniques I remember using on myself, after a session with one of my own healers.

In ESR, you hold specific neurovascular points on your forehead and then either visualise your stress or simply think about it while taking deep breaths. This technique will help you release past, present and even future stresses. Of course, we can't change the past, or tell ourselves to forget stressful memories, and we can't control the future. But we can help release any stress, fears or worries we're holding onto. That's what ESR helps you to do.

If you're reading this book, chances are you sometimes feel stressed about certain aspects of your life and find it hard to let these thoughts go. Perhaps you constantly stress about events that are yet to happen, or rerun past events through your mind in a constant, emotional loop. This is when ESR works its magic.

Most of what we find stressful in our lives results from the triggering of old emotional patterns, or by past situations that we may or may not entirely remember. But our body and subconscious mind does, say authors Charles Krebs and Tania O'Neill McGowan in *Energetic Kinesiology*.

This may mean that even small events happening to us today are affecting us on a much larger scale than we realise. If old events are triggering us to feel stressed and we don't release this, we stay stuck in a constantly stressed state, reacting from a fight or flight response, always living in survival mode.

When you start to use ESR, you can release subconscious worries so you are more easily able to choose how to act, instead of always subconsciously reacting.

ESR works by bringing blood to the frontal cortex, which allows us to think rationally and calmly. When we're in a frightened, stressed or anxious state, blood flows away from this frontal cortex to the back of our brain, towards our brain-stem-limbic survival system, which is our lizard brain, our fight or flight survival mechanism.

By holding these points on your forehead, fresh perspectives to old problems will surface, stress can be released, and you no longer need to run your life from a place of fear and reactivity.

How to use ESR

- Find a quiet, calming space.
- Think of a stressful issue. Note how your body feels. Where are you holding the stress, tension or tightness? What does it feel like in your body?
- Assess your emotional and physical energy on a scale of 1–10.
- Put your hand, palm down, across your forehead, so your pinkie finger runs along the top of your eyebrows, then hold it there lightly for the duration of this balance. If it feels easier to use both hands, then using your index and middle finger on both hands, put light pressure on your forehead a few inches above each eye, about evenly spaced between the top of your eyebrows and your hairline. (You may feel a slight indentation in your forehead.) By doing this, you're activating the emotional stress release points.
- Close your eyes and focus on the stressful event or problem that's currently going on for you. As you think of it, really get a sense of what you're feeling and worrying about, and what thoughts are running through your mind. Notice where you're feeling this in your body.
- Now start visualising how you'd like this situation to play out. See the details, colours, shapes, sounds, smells and

feelings involved. Make it real for you; run through the situation from beginning to end, in vivid detail and bold colour. You may even like to watch it in black and white too; speed it up, slow it down, whatever you need to do.

- Keep holding your hand on your forehead until you feel a shift; this may be energetic or emotional, or you may just start to feel much calmer. Perhaps you'll forget about your stress and start thinking about what's for dinner. When you feel ready, release your hand and open your eyes.
- Now recheck your body's emotional and physical energy on a scale of 1–10.
- Feel free to do this as often as you need, thinking about any stress or visualising any situation as you'd like it to play out.

How do you know when you have defused the stress?

Sometimes you'll feel pulses under your fingertips after a few seconds to a few minutes (they feel like your wrist pulses). When they become synchronised on both sides of your forehead, beating at the same time, the emotional stress defusion is complete. (As an interesting aside: ESR is also sometimes called Emotional Stress Defusion. The word 'defusion' is a term used in cognitive therapy when referring to techniques that help people distance themselves from their thoughts, similarly to when we speak about detaching from the ego in the self-development world.)

Often for me, I'll forget about the stress and start thinking about something else (which is kind of the point!). I often find my vision is so much clearer and colours are much brighter once I've opened my eyes after going through the process.

You may have to repeat this process as often as needed, or if a different version of the stress comes to mind after you've cleared the first one. That's okay; it's good to do this process whenever you need. I often suggest clients do this each night before falling asleep in the lead-up to any event they're worried about, or just until the stress they're feeling passes.

❧ How to add ESR to your toolkit ❧

The easiest way to do this is to simply start using this technique every day, or as often as you need it.

If you've been worrying about something for a while, I suggest using ESR and thinking about that particular stressful event or thought, for ten to fifteen minutes a day, for a couple of weeks. You'll see how the stress will shift, energy will move to where it's needed and new alignments will fall into place ... truly magical!

Chapter 25

balancing your chakras

ec"ec"o

efore I started to learn about the chakras, I found them incredibly overwhelming for some reason (most likely because of a block in a chakra or two!). Throughout my years as a kinesiologist though, I've gradually absorbed more and more information about the chakras and I now find them fascinating and wonderful.

Knowing how your energy affects your physical body, your emotional health and the flow or prana (life-force) of your entire life is a beautiful thing. I believe there's so much we can learn about ourselves through the chakras and, by doing so and keeping them clear and balanced, we can elevate our health, our mental and emotional wellbeing, our intuition, our vision and our psychic abilities.

The purpose of this chapter is to invite you to begin to understand how to work with the chakras in your everyday life, and to deepen your own knowledge of them in order to deepen your connection to yourself.

The chakras are energy centres throughout the body which connect us to the universe. They are our personal power centres. There are minor chakras and major chakras. We'll focus on the seven major chakras: the base, sacral, heart, solar plexus, throat, brow and crown.

Vibrating at specific frequencies, our chakras play an important role in our physical, spiritual and emotional health. Our chakras are connected to our endocrine glands and, as Richard Gerber says in *Vibrational Medicine*, the chakras are able to affect the function of our central nervous system, as well as our moods and behaviour, through hormonal influences on brain activity. He goes on to explain that because the chakras supply subtle energy to all our organs, any emotional blockages or issues can result in disrupted energy flow to any system in our body. If this energy flow is disrupted for long periods of time, it may result in an illness in any organ or system of the body, or emotional disharmony.

Let me give you an example of how your chakras and your constant comparison may be intertwining in everyday life. Imagine this: you're going through a period in your life where you're constantly feeling very unsteady and ungrounded in day-to-day activities, yourself, your relationships and your work. You're constantly feeling worried about your place in the world, stuck in fight or flight mode (anxious, exhausted, running on adrenalin), feeling that you're struggling to just survive, and you're unsure how to release the fear you're carrying around with you all day. This all relates to possible imbalances or blocks in your base chakra, also often called the root chakra.

You may be feeling creatively blocked and stagnant, as if nothing is flowing the way you want it to. You may even be suffering from hormonal imbalances and creative or sexual insecurity (sacral chakra), plus you're lacking in self-confidence and self-belief, and feeling utterly powerless in your life (solar plexus chakra). You're finding it hard to be compassionate and loving towards yourself (and sometimes even those around you). On the physical level, perhaps you're getting heart palpitations (heart chakra).

You feel like you can never really be honest with yourself about where you're at or how you're feeling; you have very little confidence about speaking up at work or with those you love. You've completely lost your unique voice in your work and sometimes, when you do try speak up, you constantly have to clear your throat or cough (throat chakra).

You also find it hard to see what's ahead of you, gain a clear perspective and have trust in your vision (brow chakra) and listening to guidance, deepening your spirituality or being supported by something greater than yourself feels completely foreign to you (crown chakra). How could you ever let go and trust when you're feeling so stuck and rooted in fear?

Now, this scenario might sound a little over the top, but I've truthfully felt most of those imbalances throughout my journey from comparison to confidence, and so have many of my clients.

When I started to truly look at how to balance and care for my chakras, I noticed huge changes and differences in my life and in how grounded, creative and nourished I felt. And even if I still felt a little unsteady or imbalanced, my acute awareness helped me heal faster and bring attention to what needed some care, some cleansing and a lot of compassion.

I've also seen firsthand the benefits in my clients' lives, once they started to work on clearing, cleansing and balancing their chakras.

From feeling ungrounded, lacking in self-confidence, not being able to see the bigger picture, speaking your truth or listening to your intuition (and so much more), when you balance your chakras and help shift energetic blocks, you truly open yourself to a higher vibration that'll touch every area of your life (and the lives of those around you). It's not magic, but the changes can be magical.

Each chakra relates to specific physical, mental, emotional and spiritual issues. So here's a brief rundown of the chakras and their elements:

Base (first chakra) ~ Grounding/safety

Red in colour, the base chakra is situated at the base of your spine and relates to your feelings of safety and security, your tribe and place in the world, basic survival (fight or flight mode), feeling grounded or rooted to the earth and easily able to make decisions on a daily basis. If you've been worrying about your basic security, whether it's to do with money, travel, relationships, where you're living or anything else, your base chakra will be involved. The base chakra relates to the reproductive system and glands. It may also relate to the adrenal glands, and the fight or flight mechanism, when you're feeling ungrounded, stressed out and unsafe. Crystals to work with in healing and balancing this chakra include red jasper, smoky quartz, garnet or hematite.

Sacral (second chakra) ~ Creativity/sexuality

Orange in colour, this chakra relates to the energies of sexual and creative power and energy, and to the genit-ourinary system and the cells of the testes and ovaries. It also relates to our external relationships with things such as money, sex, power and addictions. If this chakra is out of balance, you may be looking for control or security from things outside yourself, feeling like you can't sexually or creatively express yourself, or feeling creatively or sexually blocked and stagnant. You may also be suffering from hormonal imbalances. The crystals to work with in healing and balancing this chakra include orange calcite, yellow jasper, carnelian and sunstone.

Solar plexus (third chakra) ~ Personal power/self-worth

This chakra is yellow, located around the stomach area and relates to everything involved with **self**: self-love, self-worth, self-confidence, self-acceptance and how powerful you feel within yourself. The solar plexus is connected to the digestive system and similarly to the base chakra, the adrenal glands. Notice if you're pushing yourself to your limits to prove your personal power and if you're also suffering from fatigue and digestive issues. A great crystal to work with in healing and balancing this chakra is citrine.

Heart (fourth chakra) ~ Love/compassion/forgiveness

Green in colour, this chakra (located over your heart/chest area) carries the energies of love, self-love, love for others, compassion and forgiveness. It's connected to the circulatory system and, of course, the heart and chest area, and the thymus gland. Notice if you have any heart palpitations, a tightness or constriction in your chest area, a stagnation of blood flow such as cold hands or feet, or if you're finding it hard to receive or give love, to be compassionate or forgiving with yourself or others. You may choose to work with the crystals aventurine, emerald, green amethyst or rose quartz for this chakra.

Throat (fifth chakra) ~ Communication/will

Blue in colour, the throat chakra (located at the throat) helps us activate our voice and speak our truth. If you've been finding it hard to speak up, or say what you really mean, your throat chakra may need some clearing and balancing. It's connected to the respiratory system and the thyroid.

Notice if you're getting a sore throat or clearing your throat a lot when speaking, or if there are any thyroid imbalances. You may choose to work with the crystal blue quartz for this chakra.

Brow (sixth chakra) ~ Intuition/inner vision

Violet in colour and located at your third eye (between your eyebrows), this is about new perspectives, a clear vision, being open to seeing what's in front of you, as well as what's inside (consciousness, introspection and self-awareness) and seeing the bigger picture, as well as trusting your intuition. Imbalances can relate to sinus or eye issues, as well as endocrine imbalances. This chakra is connected to the autonomic nervous system and the pituitary gland. You may choose to work with the crystals amethyst or iolite for this chakra.

Crown (seventh chakra) ~ Spiritual seeking

Clear/white in colour, our crown chakra (just above our head) holds the energy of receiving guidance from our higher selves, angels, and the universe, and with deep inner searching. When we are balanced in our mind, body and spirit, this chakra is at its most powerful and balanced. It's connected to the central nervous system and the pineal gland. Imbalances in this chakra may manifest in lowered mental health. A crystal you may choose to work with for this chakra is clear quartz.

ᥱᥱ **Balancing your chakras** ᥤᥤ

When our chakras are out of balance, any area of our body or life may feel out of balance. Our chakras provide energetic nutrition to our body, and to the organs they relate to. To feel balanced on all levels, we must take the time and make the commitment to balance and cleanse our chakras. Luckily, there are some lovely ways we can do this through colour therapy, essential oils, meditation, movement, certain foods and more.

You may even be balancing your chakras without realising it. A little while ago, a client came in for a session and, throughout the session, it became clear there was a block in her solar plexus chakra, relating to feelings of low self-worth and low self-confidence. As we went through her kinesiology balance, I pointed out the yellow T-shirt she was wearing, and how this was essentially a colour balance for her solar plexus chakra. She burst out laughing and you could see relief flood her face. She was already using colour therapy to balance her solar plexus chakra, and she didn't even know it!

This has happened countless times over the years. A client will come in wearing a green necklace that's hanging over her heart, when she needs to work on her heart chakra; or a blue scarf around her neck, when she is working on clearing and balancing her throat chakra.

Guided chakra-cleansing meditations

This is one of my favourite ways to balance chakras. Meditation is an important method of opening, activating, balancing and cleansing the chakras, especially when practised with visualisation.

In *Vibrational Medicine*, Richard Gerber notes that with repeated chakra-cleansing guided meditations over time, a circulating current in our brain is established, which gradually releases old stresses locked into the brain tissue itself. This meditative practice allows new neural pathways to be established, preventing the accumulation of stress, and actually promoting the creation and stimulation of pleasure centres within the brain, to help maintain stress release and keep us feeling calmer and happier. How incredible and fascinating.

It's for these reasons that I offer guided meditations on my website (www.elevatevitality.com.au), and you'll find countless more online. Find one that resonates with you, then set aside some time to do it a couple of times every week (or even every day for a little while).

A lot of stuff can shift through this, so be sure to be gentle to yourself afterwards. Drink lots of water and perhaps have a cleansing Epsom salts bath, a walk in nature or by the ocean.

Chakradance

Another wonderful way to balance your chakras is to go to Chakradance classes. It's a fun and intuitive healing practice that combines music with dance, chakras and mandala art creation.

You can also chakradance at home by yourself—simply search on *Spotify* for chakra dancing tracks. Find one that resonates with you, then get dancing!

Yoga

Did you know that many yoga poses balance certain chakras? Downward dog is wonderful for the base chakra, as is tree pose (grounding, grounding, grounding!). Dancer's pose opens the heart chakra and strengthens the solar plexus chakra. And simple twists with your chin tucked in and eyes gazing upwards squeeze the thyroid and can cleanse the throat chakra, and on and on we could go. So even your daily or weekly yoga classes are working to clear, cleanse, balance and strengthen your chakras (among the bazillion other reasons why yoga is amazing).

Using crystals

You can work with the crystals mentioned for each chakra in your chakra balancing work. Simply choose which chakra you feel needs some balancing, select the appropriate crystal and then cleanse, program and work with it as outlined in Chapter 29 of this book. For instance, you may lie down to do a full chakra cleanse meditation and lay a specific crystal on their corresponding chakras.

You can also use essential oils that relate to each chakra, eat certain foods and wear the colours of the chakras.

ᘐᓂ How to add chakra balancing to your toolkit ᓂᘐ

Settle yourself in for a chakra-balancing guided meditation, go to a yoga class, wear the colour of the chakra you want to balance, or work with the crystals of the chakras.

Chapter 26

oracle and angel cards

ᴄᴦᴘ

I sought guidance from a kinesiologist who pulled oracle and angel cards before I studied kinesiology myself. I had no idea what this was all about, and the term 'angel card' made me kind of nervous. I didn't really trust that the right card would come up for me. Yet each time a card was pulled I was left speechless, or I'd burst out laughing at the beautiful synchronicity and confirmation that had unfolded before my eyes.

There is something incredibly special about what happens when you pull an angel or oracle card from a deck and it's exactly what you needed to see and hear, whether or not you consciously knew it.

When I was going through an extremely challenging time at work, being called to really step up my game, use my voice and show up more fully in my work, I went through a couple of weeks where the only thing that soothed my nerves were my oracle cards. It's not that I was trying to tell the future with them, I was just asking for guidance, connection, clarity and confirmation. Sometimes the cards that fell out of the deck would make me cry with relief, laugh with pure joy or take deep, calming, balm-like breaths, releasing stuckness and pain from deep down inside.

I would write down each card and it's reading in my journal, as a way of cementing what was being confirmed. It was a way to say, *Yes, I hear you, thank you for this guidance.*

I recently felt guided to pull a four-card reading for my newsletter list. I'd never done this before, and I didn't know if my readers would resonate with it as much as I do. Four cards pulled speak of the past, the present, the future and the best (or most appropriate) outcome. I asked my readers to let me know if they enjoyed the reading. And … I was blown away by the response. People told me stories of tears, of deep gratitude, of the cards being exactly what they needed to hear.

On your journey to confidence and personal power, you get to connect with yourself and your guidance in whatever way feels nourishing and expansive to you. One of the best ways to deepen your spirituality is to call it forth, and you can do this by working with oracle/angel cards.

ॱ How to use them ॱ

I love to pull a card to begin my day or week; it sets a beautiful new intention and energy and often gives me a message for what's to come, or what might need my attention at that time.

Sometimes a few cards will fall out of the deck, or a couple will be stuck together. Be mindful if this happens, as you're being asked to put two and two together, so to speak, and to notice the signs you're being shown in relation to the cards' messages. If you pull a card and it comes out upside down, you know there's some kind of block to the message being received and you're being called to make more space to receive its message.

To begin, choose a deck that resonates with you (I've listed my favourites for you in this chapter). Many decks give you information or guidance on how to use the cards or how to program them for your use at the beginning of the information booklet that comes with the deck, so take a few minutes to read through this.

To clear the deck of any previous energy (from the last owner or handler or just in between uses), tap or knock on the deck three times before pulling a new card.

Set the intention that the right message will come up for you, and know it's supporting you; but it's not the be-all, end-all.

I'd also like you to be mindful of the energy you bring to the deck when you're about to pull a card. If you're feeling incredibly needy (and there's nothing wrong with that) or like you just want answers and external validation, you may never feel satisfied with the message that comes up for you through the cards.

It's beautiful guidance, support and love from the universe; but you have all of that beautiful guidance, support and love inside you too. Simply ask for it to be shown to you, and it will.

How to add angel and oracle cards to your toolkit

Choose a deck to start working with, one that resonates with you. As I mentioned, I love to pull a card at the beginning of the month, week and sometimes daily too. You can use them as often as you feel you need to.

Some of my favourite cards:

- *The Little Sage Oracle Cards* by Helen Jacobs
- *The Liquid Crystal Oracle Cards*
- *Goddess Guidance Oracle Cards* by Doreen Virtue
- *Flower Therapy Oracle Cards* by Doreen Virtue
- *Healing with the Angels* by Doreen Virtue
- *Daily Guidance from Your Angels* by Doreen Virtue
- *Angels, Gods and Goddesses* by Toni Carmine Salerno
- *Universal Wisdom Oracle Cards* by Toni Carmine Salerno
- *Gaia Oracle* by Toni Carmine Salerno

Chapter 27

energetic essences, oils and sprays

༄

I used to take the Bach flower essence, Rescue Remedy, from an early age. I remember taking it before my final high school exams, and a fellow student commented that it was just a placebo effect, and that if I hadn't studied, taking an essence wouldn't help. I just smiled at this person, replying: 'I know how well this works for me. And anyway, if it **were** just a placebo effect and it allowed me to feel calmer in my exams and improved my performance, then that's a pretty great effect, right? Also, I've studied my little tush off, but thank you.'

I ended up doing incredibly well. So whether it was the Rescue Remedy, studying intensely, the little Buddha that I kept in my exam pencil case (to rub his belly for luck) or a combination of all three, I don't really mind.

Since then, I've studied Bach Flower and Australian Bush Flower essences in naturopathy college and used them in my clinic for years. After a little while, I started to add in the use of energetic and vibrational essences, which differ to flower essences in that they're created using a combination of light, sound, colour, energy, essential oils and other energetic elements. If I had to list the top few things that have helped support, protect and ground me in the past few years, the things that have allowed me to transcend what needed to be transcended, I would include energetic essences, oils and sprays in that list.

Vibrational medicines include flower essences and other energetic essences, oils and sprays. These make up a large part of the work I do with my clients, and have been a huge part of my own healing. Usually, the essences we use (or need to use) represent the attitude, mindset or intention we're needing to either release or embody, in order to feel healed and whole.

Flower essences work at the highest vibrational levels of our emotions, thought patterns, attitudes, and mindsets, which is why they can help to shift, raise and change our vibration. In *Vibrational Medicine*, Richard Gerber says: *One of the best ways to alter dysfunctional patterns in the subtle bodies is to administer therapeutic doses of frequency-specific subtle energy in the form of vibrational medicines.*

And that's the beautiful, incredible, wondrous thing about these essences; they raise our vibration and frequency at a cellular and auric level. They help us transcend and empower ourselves, and feel grounded and settled. They shift what needs shifting. They create space. They balance and heal.

Whatever is going on for you emotionally, there'll be an energetic and vibrational essence that'll help support you.

ею How to use them се

In client sessions, we use essences as part of the balance. This means an essence (or an oil or spray) might come up to clear a certain trapped emotion, to infuse a positive emotion or to simply bring more awareness to the issue at hand.

Depending on the essence (or the brand or creator's instructions) some work best if you concentrate on taking one each day until finished, while some work well in combination with other essences.

They can work to shift emotional stuff on every level. I've seen clients' energy, perspective and even their life path shift for the better, after taking some of these essences.

During the creation of huge projects I take certain essences, depending on where I'm at in the project and what I'm needing to either shift or receive. From uplifting your self-worth, confidence and motivation to helping you digest information and ideas, release loneliness, anger, resentment and fear, energetic and vibrational medicines are powerful, powerful tools that help you shift what you don't need, raise your vibration, and live from a purer, clearer, lighter state of being.

ею Healing at the heart level се

I see energetic and vibrational medicine and healing yield results time after time after time, client after client after client. And when I see the shifts come about, I know it's working on a very deep level.

If you've never tried any kind of vibrational or energetic medicine and you're a little sceptical, that's okay. Try it for yourself but **not** with the intention of proving someone else right or wrong. Try it from an open heart and a willing soul and see what shifts for you.

℅ How to add energetic essences to your toolkit ℗

You'll find my favourite essences, oils and sprays following, so I suggest doing a little bit of fun research then listening to your intuition (who totally, always knows best). Then select the ones that feel right for you.

As an example, because this book is so much about self-worth, perhaps an essence that raises your worth would be helpful, or perhaps you'll choose one that infuses confidence, or helps you listen to your inner guide.

Some of my favourite ranges of essences, oils and sprays:

- *Resonate Essences*
- *Sacred Self Alchemical Oils*
- *The Liquid Crystals*
- *Bach Flower Remedies*
- *Australian Bush Flower Essences*

Please be mindful that since the essences are shifting old stuff out, you may sometimes feel this more strongly in the first few days. When I first took the *Resonate Essences Worth* essence, I felt really low for the first few days. I couldn't work out why, until I put two and two together. Then I relished in releasing those old, pent-up emotions. So let whatever needs to be shifted go, knowing you're raising your vibration and making space for the beauty of what's to come.

Chapter 28

journaling and automatic writing

ꝏꝏ

I have already lost touch with a couple of people I used to be.

Joan Didion, on keeping a notebook

I remember my very first journal entry, when I was about ten or eleven years old. My friend was over and we were playing vets (my fluffy seal pup toy had injured itself somehow) and singing to Mariah Carey.

Since then, I've always kept a journal and I know with certainty it's helped me through some very tough times. For me, journaling does two things. Firstly, it helps me move the stressed, tired, anxious, worried or fearful (or whatever else I'm feeling) energy out of my body and into something else. My journal energetically carries everything I no longer need (as well as things I wish to manifest into my life).

Secondly, journaling helps me to see what I've been able to overcome. I can flick back through months that felt very difficult and see how strong, how brave and how resilient I was. This then inspires me to be strong, brave and resilient today.

Both journaling and automatic writing build resilience, confidence and resourcefulness; all beautiful traits we need in order to live a life imbued with self-worth and self-acceptance.

What's the difference between automatic writing and journaling?

Excellent question. Journaling is when we consciously write out what we feel needs to be written, whether it's about our day or something we're going through or worried about. Automatic writing is when we create the space to ask questions (of the universe, your higher self, inner guide, intuition, soul or whatever else you resonate with) and then let the answers pour out through you and onto the page.

Automatic writing goes a little deeper than journaling. It's more of a subconscious than conscious act; we dive deeper into our consciousness, we ask for guidance, and we let our pens scribble across the paper and unleash guidance that was hidden beneath overwhelming conscious thought.

Remember when we spoke about trust? Automatic writing instils trust in yourself when you're able to let go, write out your question or thoughts and then facilitate the answers to flow onto your page.

If you need some support with automatic writing, I highly recommend Janet Conner's book, *Writing Down Your Soul*. This resource goes beyond simply explaining what journaling and automatic writing is, and will inspire and support you to write down what needs to be released, and to connect with, and then listen to, your soul's wisdom and guidance.

How to add journaling and automatic writing to your toolkit

This is what I recommend to my clients: to begin, go and buy yourself a journal or notebook. There's no need to spend too much money on it, so you don't feel you're 'wasting it' when you use it, but you also don't want to buy the cheapest one in the store, as you want it to feel nice to write in.

Then ... sit down and write!

Yes, it's as simple (and sometimes, as challenging) as that. You may choose to set a specific time each day to write, which I never really do (unless it's for a project, such as my book!). When it comes to journaling, I'll sit down to journal when I feel I need it, when I feel the need to get some stuff off my chest that I don't necessarily want to bounce off anyone else, just myself.

Chapter 29

working with crystals

ᘓᘏᘓ

I love working with crystals, both with my clients and for myself. Crystals can help raise our energy and vibration, and can be worked with to manifest and receive, as well as let go of what we no longer need.

My dad is a diamond merchant. I remember going to his office in the school holidays and sorting semiprecious stones and diamonds (and sometimes crawling through the carpet if I dropped one on the floor!). So on some level I feel like I've been attracted to working with crystals for years.

Here's a simple process to work with them:

First, you'll want to select which crystal to work with

You can do this a few ways. When working with my clients, if a chakra comes up as blocked in our session, we'll work with the crystal that best suits that chakra. I also have crystal oracle cards that we'll pull (they're the *Liquid Crystal Oracle Cards* mentioned previously), so a client may choose to buy that crystal (or even take it as a liquid crystal essence) as a way to further their healing.

I may just get a sense I need to work with a certain crystal, or one will miraculously find its way into my life. I was on holiday in San Francisco with my husband a little while ago and as we were walking down Mission Street, we turned a corner and there stood this amazing crystal stall. A beautiful woman was selling crystal clusters of all shapes and sizes, and several chunks of amethyst called out to me. Of course, I was travelling so I couldn't buy the biggest one I saw (but oh, how I wanted to!). A big piece of aragonite jumped out at me too, which came in handy the following months, so it was really quite serendipitous (which let's be honest, is not just a beautiful word but a beautiful thing in life, too).

Then you'll want to cleanse it

We cleanse crystals so they no longer hold onto old energies, either of their past owners, handlers or from storage or shipping, or even from ourselves. Amethyst is a 'self-cleansing' crystal, so you don't need to cleanse it, although when I buy a new piece of it I'll often just cleanse it once anyway and then program it to my energy and frequency.

The simplest way to do this is to run them under purified or spring water, cleanse them in the ocean (although not all crystals do well with salty water, e.g. hematite) or use white sage. While doing this, simply set the intention that the crystal can now release all it no longer needs.

It's now time to program and work with your crystal

Programming your crystal allows you to fine-tune its frequency and vibration to work more in line with yours, allowing it to help you attract more of what you're wanting in your life.

You can always just let the crystal's natural vibration work for and through you. For instance, citrine is often used to manifest more abundance, so you could leave it at that. Or you could program your citrine to bring you an abundance of something you particularly want. I'll often program my crystals on a more emotional level. For instance if I'm working with amethyst, I'll hold it and set the intention that it'll support me in feeling clear and strong, and that I'll have a higher sense of intuition while working with it.

It's also important you continue to cleanse your crystals as you use them

I like to cleanse my crystals if they start to feel energetically full, as if they're holding onto a lot of 'stuff', or if I've been using them in specific ways for a while and I feel they could do with a good cleanse.

You may also choose to work with the cycles of the moon

I always cleanse and reprogram my crystals with new intentions at the full moon. Then I'll cleanse them at the full moon, to help let go of all I no longer need.

ᚱᚳ How to add crystals to your toolkit ᚳᚱ

When it comes to buying your crystals, you may wish to visit a crystal store (search online to see if there are any in your area) and start to have a play with them in the store, or even order online if you wish. Buying online isn't the same as 'in person' of course, because you can't see the stones or feel which one resonates with you the most. However if you're buying a bag of tumbled stones online I think it's okay, as you usually buy them by weight so you'll receive a whole bag. I prefer to choose crystal clusters in person though.

I do think it's nice to be able to hold the crystal in your hand and get a feel for it; you'll likely sense whether it's for you or not. If you're buying a bag of crystals or purchasing from someone you trust online, then I think buying online is okay. Simply set the intention that the most appropriate crystal for your highest good will be chosen and shipped out to you.

I keep certain crystals on my desk as I work, place them in the corners of my clinic room and home, and I often wear crystals in the form of necklaces or rings. There's no right or wrong way to add crystals to your energetic toolkit, simply start using them and see what works for you. By the way, if you ever lose or break a crystal, it can be a sign you no longer need it.

Chapter 30

moving and mandala meditations

e've spoke about meditation but I have another take on it I'd like to share with you. There's more than one way to meditate, and one of my favourite ways may surprise you. For instance, have you ever coloured in a mandala?

Colouring in (or even drawing them first) a mandala is a wonderful way to practise art and meditation at the same time. And don't say you're not good at art. How good were you at three years old, when just colouring in at kindergarten? I'm sure it made you pretty happy then, when you weren't worried about what anyone else thought of your art; when it was simply for the pure joy of mixing colours and seeing them create something on your page. (I recently heard that adult colouring books are one of Amazon's highest-selling categories of books. Let's bring back colouring books, I say.)

The reason I'm suggesting colouring in mandalas as form of an art meditation is because of what they represent. 'Mandala' is a Sanskrit word that loosely translates as 'circle'. It embodies the essence of wholeness and of the universe. Creating or colouring mandalas can allow you to connect with a depth of being that goes far deeper than yourself. A little while ago I sat down to colour in a mandala and barely looked up for about two hours. It was incredibly calming and meditative. When I'd finished, I had this beautiful piece of art that's now on the wall above my desk.

Another beautiful way to meditate is through movement; whether it's a long ocean walk or swim, a cycle in nature, a chakra dance, a sweaty, flow yoga class, or simply sitting in a meditation while moving your body in swaying motions that feel good to you. Listen in to your body's messages and honour what you need to do to meditate, to sit, to connect and to distil noise into knowledge and confusion into wisdom.

How to add moving and mandala meditations to your toolkit

You can look up 'mandalas to colour in' on the internet and see what comes up. Then start painting, colouring in or even drawing your own.

Chapter 31

cleansing your home and space

ᕤᘚᕤᘚᕤ

Cleansing your home and space is a wonderful way to shift old energy out and welcome in the new. Between clients, I always use white sage or an energetic spray, to shift out old energy. I also use it at the beginning and end of each working week to say 'hello' to the new week on a Monday and 'goodbye' to the working week on a Friday, ushering in the weekend.

Apart from simply setting the intention to clear the air and opening a window, there are a couple of other ways you can cleanse your home and space:

- Place small bowls of salt water in the corner of each room in your home, to absorb negative energy and cleanse the room.
- Buy a stick of white sage to cleanse your home. Simply light the end of the white sage and walk with it through

your home. (How cute, my hubby loves doing this in our home and does it all the time now.) You may intuitively get a feeling for where energy is a little heavy, stuck or stagnant, so spend extra time there.

ॐ Use energetic room clearing sprays.

ॐ Put crystals put in the corners of your rooms. Choose which crystals to put in your room depending on what's happening for you. As an example, hematite is very protective, so you may choose to put that somewhere in your office if you feel you need some extra energetic protection at work.

Just ensure that if you're using crystals, you look after them and cleanse them, using the information in Chapter 29.

How to add space clearing and cleansing to your toolkit

Go out and buy yourself a stick of white sage (found in many good health food stores) and begin to use it at home. Simply light the end of it and carry it through your home, being mindful of energy changes you feel as you walk around your home, and paying particular attention to those spaces. It can be quite a strong smell, so perhaps light only a small section of the end of the sage stick initially, as you get used to it.

You can also check out the energetic sprays I mentioned in Chapter 27, and choose whichever one resonates with you. And of course, you likely have all the ingredients for a bowl of salty water at home already.

Chapter 32

healers and therapies

❦

I truly believe we weren't meant to do everything by ourselves. I also believe there'll never be just **one** therapy, modality, food, herb or resource that will change everything for you. It's something I've taught my clients for years and they can attest to it too: there'll always be a combination of things that come together to bring about the change you desire.

One piece of this puzzle can be working with therapists, practitioners and healers, who can support you through change and help you see yourself, your world and your thoughts in a different light.

I've consulted lots of different healers and therapists through my life and some were essential in helping me overcome difficulties and transcend problems that felt insurmountable. Of course I also showed up and did the work myself (self-responsibility will always hold more weight than what someone else tells you) but I was really open to looking at and receiving others' advice, absorbing what I needed from it and releasing the rest, then taking action in whichever way felt right for me.

You may choose to seek help from a kinesiologist, a reiki healer, naturopath, psychologist, acupuncturist, or someone in a different field who feels nurturing for where you're at. I really urge you to do this if it feels right for you. And don't let a negative or less-than-best experience sway you. I once saw an osteopath who hurt me so much that I swore off osteopaths for life ... until I tried a new osteopath who was incredible, who totally understood what I needed and who re-aligned my body in the most incredible way.

If a practitioner doesn't work for you, it just means **that** practitioner doesn't work for you. It doesn't mean the therapy or the modality on the whole doesn't suit you, so keep trying until you find the person, the therapy, the modality that fits.

How to add healers and therapies to your toolkit

Nothing beats word of mouth when it comes to finding therapists and healers to support you. So ask some people in your close circle if they've seen any therapists who have helped them.

Concluding Pages

swaddle yourself in sacred support

❧

In my first year working as a naturopath, I went to a seminar on blending liquid herbal medicines. The lecturer was a well-established and highly-respected naturopath, and she was explaining how each of us might treat clients and cases differently.

She looked around the room of over fifty participants and said: 'I could give each of you the same client case study and the same herbal dispensary, and ask you to make up a herbal formula for your client. I can almost guarantee that each of you would create a different herbal formula, and I could almost guarantee that you'd all be right.'

You might sit down tomorrow and start the book you've always wanted to start; you might craft the opening lines to your first or fiftieth blog post; you might start the sketches on the design that'll get you further in your career than you ever thought possible.

Communicate and express yourself in a way that aligns with who you are, on every level. Don't let your doubts drag you down, because no matter what you do, you're right … for you.

You could sit down to write a book on self-worth, self-confidence and self-acceptance, as I've done. Yet your book will look, sound, read and feel completely different to this book you're holding in your hands. Same ideas, yet understood through different thought patterns, contexts and guidance.

Your context, your consciousness, your cells are what makes you different, unique and incredible. You are one special human. Trust that. Go with it. Raise your vibration and raise your confidence. Trust your clarity and clear your path. Open to your guidance, to your wisdom, to your knowledge. Respect yourself and release the rest, because you are enough.

ᘓᘓ The thread to weave ᘒᘒ

Even though this is the last chapter, I'd love to invite you to continue to weave a thread through everything you've learnt in this book in the coming days, weeks, months and years of your life.

- Continue to release what's not working.
- Continue to give yourself permission to be the best version of yourself.
- Continue to align yourself and use your energetic toolkit to feel more confident and worthy.

I hope what I'm conveying to you here will inspire you to pick yourself up, dust yourself off and carry on, with compassion, insight, awareness and a deep sense that you're worthy, that you're enough, that the best version of yourself is already inside you.

You don't have to add more tasks to your notepad or schedule, you don't have to stretch yourself further than you can reach, and you don't have to be someone you're not.

Address problems before they show up as scars. Cleanse and heal yourself daily, by releasing what's keeping you stuck and by balancing and aligning your energy, to create space for yourself.

Self-worth is the true essence of our being. It's our natural state. It doesn't always take a lot to shift into this state, nor does it need to take a long time. Our spiritual growth doesn't take place in linear time. You can't schedule spiritual awakening in between your 9am meeting and your midday conference call. It comes when it needs to, when you make space for it, when you're open to it. It does not come when you decide to keep improving yourself because you don't think you're worthy, but when you start accepting yourself because you **know** you're worthy.

Self-worth and self-esteem are your natural states, so each time you tell yourself you're not worthy, you're moving further and further away from the essence of who you are. When you tell yourself you're not good enough, know it's just a thought. And it can shift instantaneously; as quickly as you tell yourself that you're not worthy, you can tell yourself that you are.

The world loves who **you** are. And the sooner you see that, realise that and believe that, the sooner you'll love yourself for who you are and extend that compassion and grace into the world. The world needs you—not the tired, stressed, burnt out version of you. The world needs the best, most grounded, confident, empowered version of you. And that version of you lies inside, underneath the fear, worries, concerns, perfectionism and procrastination.

That version of you is waiting to be claimed. So I hope you'll claim it as yours, because you're so very worthy of it.

❧ The island that rose from the sea ☙

I just read a story in the newspaper about the world's newest island. It was created through massive volcanic eruptions in the Tonga archipelago, and experts say it may sink back into the ocean as quickly as it was created. This island is so new it doesn't even have a name yet.

It's fascinating that an island can just appear from ash. Looking at it, it's this beautiful black island with a small aquamarine bay. It reminded me of the Phoenix rising, of how we can create something from nothing, and of how the natural state of things just needs to be given an opportunity to come to the surface.

It made me think that no matter what your history is, you can still choose to rise today. You can decide to rise and make it happen.

You can change the course of your life by deciding to accept who you are, where you are and what is in your life, right this very moment.

You can be your own island.

You can create something beautiful from something painful or frightening, from something overwhelming or difficult. You can create whatever you want and need and crave to create.

You can be the best version of yourself, you can release yourself from the comparison trap. You can guide yourself to the highest, brightest version of health and wellness, on every level and dimension of your life.

You can do all of this ... when you accept yourself. Today.

You can be your own island.

You can make your own rules. (And then bend them and break them and let them go when you don't need them anymore.)

You can celebrate yourself today. You can.

Because **you are enough**.

i am enough affirmations

❧

se these affirmations when needed, and however they feel good to you. Remember, you can do some journaling or free writing to delve into any issues or blocks you feel in relation to these goals/affirmations, or use ESR if you feel you need to clear some stress before using them.

- ❧ *I am enough*
- ❧ *I am worthy*
- ❧ *I'm 100% aligned to owning my worth*
- ❧ *I trust my worth*
- ❧ *It's safe for me to feel worthy*
- ❧ *It's easy for me to feel worthy*
- ❧ *I'm aligned to my true purpose*
- ❧ *It's safe and easy for me to stay on my own path*
- ❧ *I easily create a future that I love*

- I release the need to compare myself to others
- I know I am enough
- I know I'm doing enough
- I'm open to receiving
- I'm abundant
- I create an abundant life for myself
- I listen to my intuition
- I follow my intuition
- I listen to my inner guide
- I embrace a deeper connection to myself
- I manifest my heart's desires
- I accept myself
- I love myself
- I am confident
- It's safe and easy for me to create what I desire
- I take action
- I am patient
- It's safe and easy for me to be patient
- I trust I'm exactly where I need to be
- I trust my path
- I have a clear vision of my future
- I easily dream about my future
- I trust I'm doing the right things

the vision manifesto

Your path is clear.

Your vision is here.

You know where you're going (even if you can't see the completed puzzle yet).

You earned it, you own it, and you claim it. (Finally. It's yours.)

You have permission to tell yourself you're good enough (more than good enough).

You know you're good enough (more than good enough).

You carve out and honour the space you need to craft, to create, to hone your skills.

Your vision is manifesting.

Your dream is coming true.

You know that Divine timing is the right timing.

And you're okay with this.

You're more than okay with this.

You trust your path, your vision, your dream and your timing.

You easily shift what's hurting, halting and holding you back.

You know you're worthy of attracting all you desire.

You know you're worthy of creating what you must create.

You know you're worthy of empowerment.

Your vision is illuminated.

Your vision is manifesting.

Your vision is yours.

Your vision is here.

a note to my (perfectionist, burnt out) reader

✼

Before I sat down to write my book, I almost scared myself out of it. Every second person who heard I was writing a book would tell me, 'Ooh that's going to be so hard! So much work! So hard!' None of these people had written their own books, so I didn't take their advice (which wasn't so much advice, as fear-based opinions). I decided I had to do one thing, and one thing only—sit down, and write. (Okay, two things.)

I thought I'd have to clear my entire schedule, never leave my house, eat random lunches at my work desk and drink cold tea, because I was too in the zone to get up and boil the kettle. I thought I'd have to say 'no' to all social invitations, and that I wouldn't be able to have a restful weekend until the book was finished.

And yet … none of this was true. I went to early morning yoga classes, barre classes, spin classes and strength classes. I sat in a cafe with a coffee most mornings and wrote, did a little more at home and then started my day from there. I had whole afternoons off, many mid-week lunch dates with girlfriends, and weekend brunches, lunches and dinners with my hubby, family and friends. My business ran as usual, as did everything else.

A friend texted the other day: *I don't know how you do it all.* I replied: *I don't do it all; I do want I want to do, what I choose to do, and what I need to do, and I say 'no' to everything else, from a place of honesty, kindness and compassion.*

Throughout this process, I didn't feel guilty if someone else thought saying 'no' was selfish. I was honest with the people in my life; if I needed to leave an event early to get to yoga, I just said it. If I was tired and needed '**me**' time, I just said it. In fact, one day a friend texted to ask if we could hang out and I replied: *Yes sure, but I need to be home by 4pm to be floppy on my bed for a bit.* She laughed, agreed she needed the same thing and we had a beautiful lunch together. Then went home separately and flopped on our own beds. Bliss!

There were a few things I did throughout the process of writing this book that you may enjoy doing too, if you're in the throes of creating something, yet your perfectionism is screaming at you: *Stop, do better! Do more! Do better, and do more of it, now!* Because I get it, and so … I'd like to help.

I sat down to write, every single day, bar a few days where I took a real rest. I aimed to write a minimum of a thousand words a day. This allowed me two things: firstly, the ability to sit down and get started every day without really pressuring myself (i.e. I didn't say, 'I'll only get up when I've finished Chapter 7', which might not have happened in a single sitting) and secondly, the ability to get up from my desk without any guilt if I **did** only write a thousand words, and not more. The pressure was off. If I wrote more, I felt happy. If I wrote a thousand, I felt happy. If I wrote a whole chapter, that was awesome. If I just flitted between chapters and finished some sentences I'd left half cooked … that was also great. And yes, some days I didn't write a thousand words at all, but luckily, the sky didn't fall.

I've never worked that way before, by setting a goal of writing a certain amount of words per day, but it worked so wonderfully for me. If you write a thousand words a day, minimum, you'll have over thirty thousand words at the end of the month. And over sixty thousand words after two months. As it worked out for me, I had almost sixty thousand words after six weeks, because the goal was light and the pressure was off.

A thousand words a day can be very easily achieved when you sit down, distraction free, eyes on the screen and heart open. Most days I could sit down between 7am and 9am to write my day's work, and then I'd still have time for all the other elements of my life and business.

The day I sat down to start my book, I snapped a pic of the exciting shenanigans and put it on Instagram, tagging one of my favourite authors, Todd Henry. It was through reading one of his books, *The Accidental Creative*, that I picked up this habit of writing a thousand words a day, so I mentioned this in my post. Todd replied almost instantly, giving me the best book-writing advice I've received to date: *No-one writes a book, they only write sections that later become a book.* This advice fuelled me every time I felt overwhelmed and, in fact, **because** of this advice I can honestly say I rarely felt overwhelmed at the task ahead, because I just saw the little steps, and the little steps felt manageable.

I wrote and wrote and wrote, didn't look at my manuscript for a couple of weeks, then sat down to polish it. In fact I took myself off to Byron Bay, up the east coast of Australia, for a solo three-day editing retreat (which is where I am as I type these words to you; it's one of my favourite places ever). That was one of the best things I could have done. I gave myself real space, expectation free, and it was beautiful. So was the coffee.

Your inner perfectionist might ask you to edit as you write, to restructure, reshape and reform your paragraphs and chapters, before you even know what they look like. But your inner ally can see the bigger picture before you do. Your inner ally wants you to get out the messiest, chunkiest first draft ever, take some space in between and then dive in with a big mug of hot tea, a pen behind your ear (you probably won't need it, but you'll look so Pinterest-ready), comfy clothes on and chilled tunes playing, so you can edit to your heart's content.

So you see, you can follow your dream and write your book (or do whatever else it is you want to do) while feeling full, whole and replete.

You can care for yourself deeply, on all levels, and still make stuff happen. Really, it's only **when** you care for yourself deeply on all levels that the **real** stuff happens anyway.

Peace out.

Cass x

acknowledgements

Firstly, thank you to everyone at Hay House; I wouldn't be writing this if it weren't for you. Thank you Leon Nacson, thank you for giving me this chance. I'll never forget the moment I picked up the phone and heard your voice, *'Hi, it's Leon from Hay House.'* That's what dreams are made of! To Rosie Barry, thank you for your generosity, your kindness, your feedback, your support and your patience. I feel so blessed to have you on my team (or rather, to be on **your** team). To Freya Thomasson, Errin Dunn, Rhett Nacson, Eli Nacson, and Margie Tubbs; thank you so much for helping to make this process as smooth and enjoyable as possible. What an absolute dream this has been! #dreamteam.

To Alice Nicholls, thank you for saying yes to writing the foreword, for your incredible support, and for your emails that make me laugh out loud. You pretty much had me at 'hello'. You are so very funny, kind, clever and inspiring. I am honoured to know you, to share this journey with you, and to have your words in the front of my book. Thank you.

To my beautiful friends whose love, friendship and support I honour and cherish, and who've been so supportive throughout this process; Bryoni Stander, Julia Tockar, Ali Gordon, Melissa Polovin, Jodi York, Jordanna Levin, Kerry Rowett, Cara Phillips, Kristin Golding, Elise Grauer, Libby Babet, Sara Brooke, Louise Jeckells, Simone McCann, Margot Macdonald, Leah Kelly, Anya Spicer, Janette Brown, and Connie Chapman. Thank you.

Dani Hunt from Neverland Studio, thank you for absolutely everything over the past few years, and for the lovingly crafted and gorgeously designed book cover. I'm so lucky to know you and work with you. I treasure our friendship and work relationship, and I can't wait to see what we continue to create together.

I'm incredibly grateful to have connected with some amazing women and healers who've supported, inspired and guided me on my journey so far, and throughout the writing of this book; thank you to Helen Jacobs, Claire Thomas, and Rachelle Sewell.

Thank you to my fellow Hay House Writer's Workshop co-winner, Celina Gregory, for being such a lovely support. Going through this experience for the first time, at the same time, has been so much fun. How lucky are we? And thank you to Megan Dalla-Camina, another fellow Hay House author, for your gentle nudge to just submit the proposal, because really ... you gotta be in it, to win it. Wasn't that a life-changing email exchange?

To my clients and readers, thank you for coming along on this journey with me! Thank you for working with me, trusting me, inspiring me, and making me laugh and cry right alongside you. Thank you for inviting me into your lives. I am so very grateful to you for being here, and deeply appreciative of your support.

To the people I consider mentors (whether they realise it or not!): Danielle LaPorte and Linda Sivertsen, for guiding me to write a winning book proposal through their multimedia program, *Your Big Beautiful Book Plan*. Danielle, it's hard to put into words how I feel when I read your work, or think of how much you inspire me through everything you do, so I'll keep it simple; *thank you*. To Melissa Cassera for reminding me it's about joy and pleasure, and not the numbers. To Alexandra Franzen for creating the space in your Sydney workshop to allow me to find my voice and call myself a writer. You don't know how much that helped me. Thank you. To Todd Henry, for your inspiring books that reminded me of my deep desire to create something everyday, and by replying to my Instagram comment with the best book-writing advice I've received so far, 'No one writes a book – they only write sections that eventually become a book.' That's on a very important post-it. Thank you.

To the crew at Sensory Lab, Bondi. Imagine how different this book would be if you hadn't made my coffee each morning? I. Can't. Even. You're all wonderful, thank you.

Thank you to my in-laws, Judy and Phil, for always being so supportive and loving, and to Jess, Daniel and Ollie; thank you for all your support, always. This will be the first book Ollie reads, right? I love you all.

To my entire extended family, my grandparents Jackie and Lollie, and to all my amazing aunts, uncles, and cousins; thank you for all of your support, and the constant laughs. I love you all dearly.

To my mum and dad, Marylou and Robin. I don't know where I'd be if it weren't for your unconditional love and support. You helped me believe I could do anything and be anything. You believed me when I said I'd be an author when I was twelve years old. You believed in me, no matter what, and supported me through everything. I can't even put into words my love and gratitude for you. I feel like the luckiest girl in the world to have you as my parents. I love you both so much. Thank you.

To my sisters, Steph and Sami. You are my entire world in my heart. So. Full. I love you more than I could ever express. Thank you for making my life better, just by being in it. And to your loves, Daniel and Gabe, I love you guys. Thank you for all your support.

To Miso, some people would think it's silly to thank a dog in my book ... but I'm not one of those people! The way we all love you is palpable. You make us all remember that we're enough, every moment we're with you.

To my hubby, Nic. My best friend, my heart, my biggest cheerleader, my lawyer, my personal chef, my tea-maker.

Thank you for believing in me and supporting me through absolutely everything, for knowing me better than I know myself sometimes, for being who you are, and for loving me unconditionally and endlessly. I couldn't love you more, but I'll try everyday until forever.

connect with cass

ᏇᎧᎧᎧᏇ

I'd love to know how you went reading this book, and what insights or changes came into play for you. Please feel free to email me through my website. You can also come find me on social media and let me know. (My favourite place is Instagram.) You can use the hashtag #UAreEnoughBook.

This is where I hang out online
- Instagram: @cassiemendozajones
- Facebook: /elevate.vitality
- Pinterest: /cmendozajones
- Twitter: @cmendozajones

If you'd like even more support, we can work together in a number of ways
Subscribe to my newsletter to receive free updates and insights at **www.elevatevitality.com.au/subscribe**.

I'd love to invite you to join my *Heartfelt Harmony*®
Society. It's a selection of lifestyle and business courses and
guides, which will help you live in freedom and harmony
every day. Visit **www.heartfeltharmony.com** for more details
and to join.

You can join my *Cleansed eCourse* to cleanse your body,
mind, spirit and space, and to shift and release what's keeping
you stuck at **www.elevatevitality.com.au/cleansed**.

If you're looking for more personalised support, we can
work together in 1:1 sessions. Find more information at
www.elevatevitality.com.au/1-1-sessions.

I also offer meditations, ebooks, free resources and more
on my website. Visit **www.elevatevitality.com.au/shop** to
download them.

If you'd like some support to help you start writing, plus
some insights into how I wrote the proposal that won me this
book deal and other insights into my writing and publishing
journey so far, visit **www.elevatevitality.com.au/writing-tips**.

For an up-to-date list of my favourite resources (some
of which have been mentioned in this book), including
courses, books, blogs, healers, podcasts and more, visit
www.elevatevitality.com.au/resources.

about the author

❦

As a kinesiologist, naturopath, author and speaker, Cassie Mendoza-Jones helps women upgrade their health and their life. She works with women who feel stuck, unworthy and disconnected from themselves.

She shows them how to increase their self-care, self-worth and self-acceptance on every level, while making it all feel like it's the most natural thing in the world. (Truth: it can be.)

When she's not working with clients, writing or creating online courses and programs, she's getting lost in a good novel, hanging out in a cafe or suiting up for a yoga class.

Meet Cassie and get ready to find the most balanced, centred version of yourself at: **www.elevatevitality.com.au**

We hope you enjoyed this Hay House book. If you'd like to receive our online catalog featuring additional information on Hay House and products, or if you'd like to find out more about the Hay Foundation, please contact:

Hay House, Inc., P.O. Box 5100, Carlsbad, CA 92018-5100
(760) 431-7695 or (800) 654-5126
(760) 431-6948 (fax) or (800) 650-5115 (fax)
www.hayhouse.com® • www.hayfoundation.org

Published and distributed in Australia by: Hay House Australia Pty. Ltd.,
18/36 Ralph St., Alexandria NSW 2015
Phone: 612-9669-4299 • *Fax:* 612-9669-4144 • www.hayhouse.com.au

Published and distributed in the United Kingdom by:
Hay House UK, Ltd., Astley House, 33 Notting Hill Gate, London W11 3JQ
Phone: 44-20-3675-2450 • *Fax:* 44-20-3675-2451 • www.hayhouse.co.uk

Published and distributed in the Republic of South Africa by:
Hay House SA (Pty), Ltd., P.O. Box 990, Witkoppen 2068
info@hayhouse.co.za • www.hayhouse.co.za

Published in India by: Hay House Publishers India,
Muskaan Complex, Plot No. 3, B-2, Vasant Kunj, New Delhi 110 070
Phone: 91-11-4176-1620 • *Fax:* 91-11-4176-1630 • www.hayhouse.co.in

Distributed in Canada by: Raincoast Books,
2440 Viking Way, Richmond, B.C. V6V 1N2 •
Phone: 1-800-663-5714 • *Fax:* 1-800-565-3770 • www.raincoast.com

Take Your Soul on a Vacation

Visit www.HealYourLife.com® to regroup,
recharge, and reconnect with your own magnificence.
Featuring blogs, mind-body-spirit news, and life-changing
wisdom from Louise Hay and friends.

Visit www.HealYourLife.com today

Printed in the United States
By Bookmasters